D0971584

ALL I SAID WAS. . . . .

Warmest Good wishes
Paul Molloy

Paul Molloy

All I said was....................

Doubleday & Company, Inc.
Garden City, New York

1966

Library of Congress Catalog Card Number 66-15668

Printed in the United States of America
First Edition

To my sister Dale
for her continuous and unwavering faith in me
that began when we were children.

It just isn't true that I dislike all newspapermen. Now take Paul Molloy. The first time I met him I wanted to punch him right in the nose.

It happened about the second year when I was doing the "Tonight" show. Then it wasn't really a show but was more like an hour and three quarters of interruptions with time out to remove the wounded. I had been described as sounding like a Methodist minister after four martinis. Well, one night I had taken on a well-known television magazine that had just printed a long story containing complete falsehoods. In my naïve, midwestern way I called them liars and worse. The studio audience loved every moment of my attack, as no one at that time had ever taken on a powerful magazine. I went on to say that unless the magazine retracted what they knew to be untruths I had a small bomb to throw about the family that published the magazine. It was quite a moment.

What I didn't know was that that night in the audience were four or five television newspapermen who were visiting New York. It appeared to them that I had done this for effect to win their support against a magazine. Later that evening, or more correctly early the next morning, I offered to meet with them, if they wished, and explain further my position. Well, the four newspapermen grew into a crowd of about twenty who came to throw verbal darts at me. It was quite unpleasant. Although I gave them back the best I could, I was outnumbered.

But there was one guy there who asked all the tough questions. He kept hitting away at me, and I wondered what had I ever done to deserve his wrath. I asked later who was the columnist in the back. I was told it was Paul Molloy. I had never met him or even heard of him. Later when the columns were written it was my first surprise with newspapermen. Paul Molloy was the only one who believed me or quoted me accurately. I am glad that I didn't punch him in the nose because any guy that honest would probably hit me back. Then, when I learned he had eight children I realized he was as unpredictable as his wife Helen later said he was. And she should know!

Well, the magazine two weeks later retracted the story, and I had a residual friend in Molloy. Although we didn't meet again for two years, I began to read his columns. Many times he criticized my work, and many times he was right. Then came the Berlin Wall story that was front-page news for three days across the country. And portions of the press of this country thought at last they had Paar right where they wanted him—out of business. This was the lowest moment of my life because I was in Europe and later Russia and couldn't answer back. There was more than a week of character assassination and falsehoods. My own mother was ready to revoke my birth certificate.

Then three weeks later the United States Army, the Federal Communications Commission, and an investigating body of the United States Senate finally came to the conclusion that I had not in any way acted improperly. Many newspapers had to take back their stories and opinions, but when I returned to the United States and read all the columns, Molloy was one of the few who got it right the first time. He judged me from what he saw me do, not from what he had heard I had done.

We now see each other when he's in New York. He has a lovely wife and enough handsome children to keep Bobby Kennedy on his toes. He is my friend and I wish him well in all his projects. He is a damn good writer, a fine father and husband, a decent, honest man. I am so glad I never hit him on the nose.

Jack Paar

Some days, it's better to stay home

An open letter to my son:

Dear Paul,

Well, this is it—your last weekend at home. On Sunday, your chair at the dinner table will be vacant and you'll be finding your way around the campus of Marquette University in Milwaukee.

And so, inexorably, the first one leaves the nest. We've kidded about that, but now the time for departure is here and I'm out of laughs. You know the pride your mother and I share as you go off to college, but with that pride I feel melancholy in my heart.

This isn't one of those advice letters from Old Dad. We hope we took care of that over the years since you crossed your first street on that first tricycle.

It's just that it's been a time of remembering, and suddenly all of the little things and the big things rush by like a strange, speeded-up film, and a father wishes he could stop each scene and play it over again. So many happenings . . . so many intimate conversations together . . . so many wordless looks that mean so much because they remain etched in the mirror of the mind. The days of the boy are over, and the days of the man are here. How could it all have raced by with such cruel swiftness? It has to be, this letting go, but letting go, Paul, just isn't easy.

I know you sensed it too, because these recent months I found you bringing up the things of the past—and it's a little odd for a teen-ager to look back. Just the other night—remember?—you brought me that picture snapped by a street photographer, and we laughed at your short pants and the way you were tugging at my hand. Then you talked about that first day of school in New Jersey.

So much to remember—and you did . . . The accident, when we thought you'd lose an eye . . . The moments when you sat in my lap and thought you were actually steering the car . . . That first plane trip . . . The day Mother came home with the first pair of long pants . . . The day you got your first hit in Little League baseball . . . And then making the All-Star team . . . And the time you sat in an audience and for the first time watched Old Dad make a speech.

And just the other night at Comiskey Park, you looked back again and talked about the first time I'd taken you to a Major League ball game. You asked if I remembered, too—as if a father could forget a delicious moment like that one.

And then suddenly the time of the little boy was gone. Now it was American Legion baseball, and I guess I started feeling a little bit old that morning when I took you for your driving test—and now you had the car, and we started having just a little bit less of you.

And one night you took extra long in the shower and combing your hair, and it was the night of the first date.

And then the change was unmistakable: Not much time, now, for television, and you began to smile at the things that once thrilled you on the screen. And I began to notice that you were reading more, and asking more questions about history and politics (and I hated myself for the ones I couldn't answer). And all of a sudden—everything's been so sudden—you were standing self-consciously in your graduation robe, and high school was over.

Now the times together were less, and I guess that's why I cherish them so. And—don't laugh—I'll always cherish those interludes late at night when the others were in bed and we'd indulge my weakness, those science-fiction things on television's "Late Show" . . . Laughing at the silliness of it all, and sometimes just sitting there together, in silence, in the living room. This I'll miss an awful lot.

And now you're going. Maybe it's corny for a father to write like this, but so be it. It's been great having you with us for a little time, because we love you so much. And I dread the night when, from habit, I'll turn on your bedroom light to look in—and you won't be there. Some day, sadly, you'll know what the feeling is. For love is like that.

And for a father, it's going to seem a long, long time until Christmas vacation brings you back for a little while.

●●●●●●●●●●●●●●●●●●●●●●

Whenever I see one of those private eyes on television, I remember George and my one experience with a private detective some years ago.

George had been working for me for a few months but I had had to fire him for gross insubordination. He retaliated by crashing into my office at 2 A.M., upsetting the desks, and making off with a set of keys that included one to my home. On my desk he left a note that said: "You'll be sorry."

I didn't want to involve the police. But he was a hard-drinking neurotic, and I had two children at the time, and I was worried. I took my fears to a private eye who occupied a cluttered cubbyhole in a neighboring block, a cadaverous fellow with wild sheaves of the reddest hair I'd ever seen.

"He sounds dangerous," the detective said. "We've got to get your keys back. You'll be the decoy. I'll go through his room while you keep his landlady busy. I can case a room in ninety seconds flat."

We had no search warrant, of course. After establishing that George wasn't home, I was to lure the landlady to the front porch on the pretext of wanting to rent a room. The intrepid one, meanwhile, would scoot up the back way.

The plan went well until the landlady grabbed my arm and all but pulled me inside. "I've got a real nice room that'll soon be vacant," she said. "The gentleman will be leaving any day, I'm sure."

"But I don't want to see it now," I protested.

"But you must," she persisted. "Come along, now."

"I'll come back tomorrow," I stammered. But now she was dragging me upstairs. Suddenly we were at the top and she threw open the door and the smile froze on her face and she uttered a banshee shriek. Before us was the bent-over posterior of the private eye, his shaggy head burrowed into a drawer and his hand scooping out shirts and socks to the left and right.

"What are you doing here?" she screamed.

My operator, a set of long underwear dangling from one hand, raised himself with as much dignity as was possible. "Madam," he said, "I must have the wrong house." With that he brushed hurriedly past her and flew down the stairs, his absurd crimson mane flying behind him. The landlady glared at me.

"You're together on this!" she shouted. "You're thieves! I'm going to call the police!"

I must have gone down those steps four at a time, panicked at the thought of getting myself arrested and embarrassing my employers. Outside I found my friend nudging his car slowly down the street, waiting for me to catch up.

"The least you could do," I puffed, jumping in beside him, "was wait for me."

"You had nothing to lose," he said, gunning the car. "I could have lost my license." Then his scrawny face broke into a triumphant smile. "Anyway, I can tell you the keys ain't there. I went over every inch."

"Has it occurred to you," I said, "that he probably has the keys on him?"

"By golly," he said, "you might just have something there. What you need is twenty-four-hour protection."

"But that's expensive," I said.

"Twenty-five dollars a day," he said, "but this guy may be off his rocker, and you've got to think of your wife and kids."

I thought. Then I said: "When can you start?"

"I'll be at your house in an hour," he said.

I had kept the unpleasantness from my wife, but now it was necessary to tell her. What vexed her was the inconvenience of a stranger sleeping on the living-room couch.

When he arrived at our home to take over his vigil, he had with him a small gray bag from which he removed a change of clothes, his shaving equipment, four confession magazines, and a vicious-looking, dark-greenish blackjack. My wife shuddered at the sight of the weapon, but he tapped it into the palm of his hand and said: "Don't worry. You'll be safe with this around." Then he slipped it into his back pocket and said: "I usually have supper at five."

Since I'd been away most of the day from the office, I worked late that night and came home shortly after midnight. As I walked along the lightless street to our front walk, an upstairs window flew open and a voice rang out. "Stay where you are, mister, or I'll shoot!"

I looked up and there was that scarlet mop hanging from the window. "For heaven's sakes, don't be so dramatic," I said. "You're supposed to watch for a fat man."

This was typical of his efficiency during the three days he stayed with us.

He was supposed to take naps during the day so he could stand watch at night, but he complained that the children kept him awake. As a result, when I'd check to see how the fort was holding in the middle of the night, I'd find him sprawled on the couch, making vulgar snoring voices.

He was forever munching on something from the kitchen —apples, bananas, even cold wieners—and once he told my wife that if she didn't mind he wasn't getting enough butter on his Brussels sprouts.

On the second night, just before we retired, he was sitting with a cheese sandwich in one hand and one of his silly magazines in the other, when a nearby cat let out a crescendo mating moan in the blackness outside. The sandwich and magazine flew out of his hands and he practically fell off the couch. "I can't stand cats," he muttered, straightening himself up. "They give me the willies."

On the morning of the third night I received an airmail letter from the man who had caused me all this dismay. It was humbly apologetic, and he explained that he had become lonesome and had flown home to another city without even bothering to pick up his personal belongings. My keys would follow by parcel post, and would I send him his personal effects?

Promptly I phoned home and told my private eye that we'd need him no longer. As he packed his little gray bag he told my wife: "You know, I've enjoyed this. It's the most exciting case I've ever had." It developed that since opening up shop he had done little beyond serve process papers, shadow a man in a divorce case, and find a pregnant girl who was hiding with friends.

Ten days later I received his bill for $75, with no deductions for board and room.

So I'm often intrigued by television's private eyes in their exotic, $400-a-month apartments, surrounded by gorgeous dolls and gallons of booze, solving all those complicated cases.

Funniest thing on the living-room screen.

•••••••••••••••••••••

On this glorious Fourth of July you're likely headed for the (ha-ha) open road, or the beach or some snazzy restaurant. Me, I'm staying home. Independence Day happens to be my birthday, and I'm flat broke.

I'm flat broke because the bills have just come in on the presents I got on Father's Day. When you have eight children, you get a lot of presents on Father's Day. And when Father's Day and father's birthday are just a couple of weeks apart—and the little ones would rather give you a tie ($2.50) than shaving lotion (forty-nine cents)—you find yourself counting the hours to payday.

What makes it disastrous at my house is that my wife's birthday comes just twenty days after mine, and Paul, Jr.'s birthday follows two days later. Right there that blows the whole July bit.

Because of our own private population explosion, this birthday business can become a small catastrophe. Another rough session occurs in February, which is known at my house as Black February.

Georgia's birthday is on February 3. Barbara's birthday is on February 4, and Marcia's birthday is on February 10. I could get through Black February all right if we could simply lock the doors, nail down the windows, dance around the cake and kiss the happy subjects. But a birthday means a party, and a party means a lot of little people with large stomachs.

Let's say Georgia invites eight friends to her party. Fine. But she has to invite her own brothers and sisters too. Now the guests number fifteen. But her own brothers and sisters see this as a chance to catch up on their own social obligations. Like Shonagh will tell Georgia: "My birthday isn't till June, but I owe parties to Carol and Fran. If you let them come to your party, you can have two of YOUR friends at MY party."

And Paul, Jr. will tell her: "You've owed me fifty cents since Christmas. If I can bring Dennis and Chip and Ted to your party, we'll call it even."

Did you ever transport twenty-three children to a Saturday matinee? And then drive most of them home—including four of the smaller ones who've forgotten where they live?

But hosting these junior bashes isn't the worst problem. Guesting is.

You see—you have eight youngsters and you can figure that each one has six or seven "best friends." That means they'll be invited to something like fifty birthday parties during the year (not counting the special parties like Easter and Halloween). But at each of these parties your children make four or five new "best friends"; and these new "best friends," they throw parties too. And it goes on and on like that, the parties multiplying until one day you look at your wife and you say: "Whatever happened to Nelda? I haven't seen her since last weekend."

Now when you and I were young, Marmaduke, we went to a party with a ten-cent present under our arm (the rich snobs plunged for a quarter). Nowadays when your child takes a gift to a party you know you'll be relieved of at least two dollars.

So you multiply eight children by fifty parties by two dollars, and you know that two days after Father's Day and two days after your birthday you're going to walk into the store with the ties and shirts, and you'll tell the man they're not the right color or style and could you please have your money back.

By last fall the whole thing had gotten out of hand—out of pocket, really—and I told the children we'd have to go very easy on Christmas. And then Nelda reminded me:

Christmas Day is also Mark's birthday.

In recent weeks I've put the torch to so many birthday candles I feel like the original lamplighter, and our house smells like a fireman's pullovers. But never mind that. I always get a kick out of kiddie parties. In fact, I get several kicks—around the shins and ankles, depending on how tall the little guests are.

It's fun all the way—from the greetings at the door ("Come on in and where's my present?") to the fond farewells ("I hate you and your stupid parties!"). Perhaps, like me, you've categorized your bubblegum brigade. I've found that at least one of the following is sure to be at any party:

The Misanthrope: This is the anti-social tyke who won't do anything. Won't play games. Won't sing. Won't watch television. Won't talk. Won't even eat. Has a perfectly miserable time. But when the party's over, he or she won't go home. Has to be forcibly removed, kicking and screaming, to the parental car outside.

The Investigator: This is the little character who's forever straying from where the action is. He wanders into all the rooms, opening drawers, inspecting cupboards, poking into wastebaskets, and nipping at the soft-drink supply (you must hide the liquor). He can often be found in the master bedroom, rummaging through Mother's underclothes.

Little Sir Kidney: No party is complete without this specimen who heads for the bathroom the moment he comes through the door. He's out to smash the all-time toilet-flushing record (which now stands at five times in one minute).

Not quite as anti-social as The Misanthrope, he speaks but two words all afternoon: "Gotta go."

The Indian Giver: You must be careful with this one, for she has been known to become violent. Within ten minutes of arrival, she develops an overpowering urge to repossess the gift she brought to the guest of honor. Nothing else will do. She goes home, then, and tells her mother the gift was rejected. Her mother will not speak to you for weeks.

The Absent-minded Professor: Watch this one. Real tricky. He begins by losing his galoshes and goes on from there—mittens, scarf, the braces on his teeth, party favors, eyeglasses, and eventually his sense of direction. Sometimes he will join Little Sir Kidney in the bathroom and manage to lose his pants. When his mother calls for him, there's an all-out search going on throughout the house, and his mother concludes that your wife is a sloppy housekeeper.

Connie Contrary: An odd one. When it's spin-the-bottle time, she's busy with jacks. When it's time to eat, she's outside on the swings and won't come in. When the other kids are singing "Happy Birthday," she obliges with "Jesus Loves Me." When it's time for stories, she wants to eat. But leave her alone. She's probably the happiest of the bunch. And when it's time to go home you'll find her, bless her contrary little soul, sound asleep on your bed.

The Weeper: A must at every party. He or she arrives in tears and cries constantly. A gentle try to ease the misery will reward you with a terribly stiff thumb in the eye. Why is he or she crying? Because it's not his or her party, that's why.

●●●●●●●●●●●●●●●●●●●●●●

"This living-room wall," said the man, peering through the movie camera, "will have to come down."

"It will?" said my wife, her voice cracking a little. Wives tend to get sentimental about living-room walls and things like that.

"Yes," said the other man. "But we'll put it back in when we're through. And we'll have to repaint your kitchen and dinette, 'cause these colors will never do. But we'll have them back in their original colors when we're finished."

The man was Robert Senglaub, movie director for the film division of General Motors Corporation. The other man was John Irvine, GM's movie producer.

So the wall came tumbling down in order that the big cameras could poke into the kitchen; and the painters moved in and the colors changed in the other rooms; and the lighting crew affixed the huge, hot lights to the ceiling, and they pasted stuff on the windows to filter the sunlight; and the sound men laid the cables along the hall and through the bathroom; and the prop men put chalk marks on the floor to indicate where we were to stand; and Helen took her place, and I took mine, and the eight youngsters stood by awaiting their cues; and someone ran up and patted the perspiration on our foreheads; and Senglaub waved to the cameras, and they started to turn, and GM's thirty-minute color *Test Site* was under way.

It all started some time back when an executive of GM's Frigidaire Division happened to read about a book I'd written, *And Then There Were Eight* (about the eight children) and, curious, bought it the next morning. After reading it he telephoned from Detroit with this proposal: Would the ten Molloys test Frigidaire's next-year washer and dryer for a few weeks, then "star" in a trade movie about the experience?

I agreed tentatively, and seven Frigidaire executives flew into Chicago and came to our suburban home to study the setup. They also brought a shooting script with them. I liked the script, they liked the children and the appearance of the home and neighborhood for film purposes, and the project was on. It was, to put it mildly, quite an experience.

I was amazed at the manner in which the children threw themselves into their roles. There is a little ham in all of us, even at a tender age.

Indeed, Barbara at one point went into a pique because, she pouted, she hadn't been given enough lines to speak. Theatrical temperament—at the age of four . . .

At another point, Lisa (six) turned to Senglaub and trilled: "I forgot my line. Would you give me my clue?" (She meant cue, but she was close.)

And once I heard Paul, Jr. tell a friend: "I can't go to (baseball) practice. We're shooting my big scene tonight."

(My cue . . . my big scene . . . Good grief, they were already sounding like Barrymores.)

Once Mark, who's three, apparently "froze" on his line during an outdoor scene in the front yard. Senglaub, who had coached him for a half-hour (Mark was having trouble with the word "refrigerator"), gave him an icy stare. Whereupon Mark, hands on hips, gave him an even icier stare. "You," he growled, "didn't say 'Action!!'" Senglaub had, indeed, forgotten to bark the command.

In one scene, Paul, Jr. had to drop a table tennis ball into the washing machine to demonstrate to me the flow of the churning water. A couple of weeks later I caught Mark waddling into the kitchen with the family basketball in his arms. He was headed for the washer, hoping to drop it in. "I couldn't," he huffed, "find the ping-pong."

The little ones have a new game now, called "making movies." Marcia gives careful instructions to Lisa, Barbara, and Mark, then snaps: "Scene 12, take 2! Action!" Despite endless flubs she always winds up with: "Cut! Let's print that one!"

Some few months later, when the movie was edited and ready for showing, the Frigidaire people took us to company headquarters in Dayton, Ohio, for a personal appearance at the "premiere" of the film before hundreds of dealers and distributors. And that's when I learned that it isn't easy to make clever conversation with a vice-president of General Motors Corporation when his nose is being tweaked.

That was the unnerving sidelight to my first meeting with the GM executive, Herman H. Lehman, who also happens to be general manager of the corporation's Frigidaire Division.

It happens that Mark likes to tweak my nose—possibly because I have a lot of nose to tweak. In return, I sometimes jab him with friendly uppercuts. So when Lehman swept him up in his arms as we were introduced, Mark promptly tweaked his nose. He also gave the man a couple of friendly jabs, all the while laughing fit to die. One of the jabs was so friendly you could hear it clear across the room.

I was a little edgy. Polishing the brass is all right, but slapping it around is something else again.

But things turned out fine, because Lehman is the dedicated grandfather of several little Lehmans. He and Mark retired to a corner and were soon engrossed in animated conversation about—I suppose—what's good for General Motors and for the country and for three-year-olds.

We drove the 650 miles to and from Dayton, which can be a problem with ten in the tonneau. To ease the crowdedness, I make the youngsters breathe in relays: When Paul, Georgia, Shonagh, and Nelda are inhaling, Marcia, Lisa, Barbara, and Mark are permitted to exhale. Without this system the doors fall off.

Several odd things occurred during the filming of the

movie. But one big jolt occurred about a week after the lensing was over. The producers had discovered that the noise of a passing plane had ruined a scene which featured my wife. The scene had to be reshot. But it developed that in the interval my wife had acquired a new hairdo. So she had to have her hair redone precisely as it had been the week before. I prefer not to recollect that day.

The movie was premiered by five hundred GM executives, dealers, and distributors, and our personal appearance as the film faded out was to be a surprise. The children were to bounce onstage for a little bit of business, then the curtain was to drop and Mark would "disappear" before it rose again.

The idea was that the stage manager was to whisk him up after the curtain had dropped, race madly out of sight through a secret passage and release him at the back of the auditorium (for him to make his way back to the stage munching a cookie).

We had about four rehearsals the night before, and finally I asked the man: "Doesn't all that piggyback stuff tire you?" Said he: "I don't (puff) mind that so (puff) much, but he keeps (puff) whacking me on the (puff) back and yelling: 'FASTER! FASTER! And the last time out he said: 'This time let's giddyap to the baf'room—I'm in a hurry.'"

The Frigidaire folks had arranged for us to be guests on television shows in Dayton and Cincinnati, including the program of Dayton TV star Joe Longstreth. Interviewing ten people, eight of them kids, is a Trojan task, but Longstreth came through beautifully. He asked them their ages and what they liked most about school ("The lunch part," said Nelda, who must have read the Joe Miller Joke Book).

Toward the end of the program Mark tugged at Longstreth's sleeve and exclaimed: "You didn't ask Mommy and Daddy how old THEY are!"

I was never happier to see a program host announce that it was time for a commercial.

•••••••••••••••••••••

One day the boy who bears my name came home with half a dozen books of raffle tickets for an excellent cause. It happens that I don't believe in children as door-to-door peddlers, and one reason is self-defense: If my eight youngsters were to fan out across the neighborhood with tickets (and cookies and such), it could spawn a massive retaliation ("You buy my son's stuff and I'll buy your son's stuff").

Anyway, the front of these raffle books bore the legend: "Donation—$2.00," and they seemed to be the ten-to-a-book kind. Since twenty cents appeared to be a small risk for the grand prize, a convertible, I decided to dispose of them at the office (a practice I do not commend).

I sold four books within water-cooler distance of my desk and was happily denuding the fifth when the *Sun-Times* sports editor, Dick Hackenberg, paused in mid-pocket and said: "Twenty cents a chance for a car? You sure this is all right?"

Sadly, it wasn't. I'd mistaken the top ticket for the book cover and assumed that the cost per book was $2.00, when actually the tariff was $2.00 a ticket. I did a lot of back-pedaling that day, leaning to leeward with a pocketful of dimes.

This small calamity got me to wondering whether it isn't time to pull the children off the streets and end the half-pint hawking whereby more and more adults are conveniently shirking their own responsibilities. There's been quite an increase in the use of children as salesmen for numerous charity causes and community projects. Looking for something in the utility closet one day, I came across boxes of Christmas cards that will—let's see—see me through 1967.

It's difficult to turn down a child, hence people often buy items they don't want for causes in which they're not interested. Since some of these projects are less worthy than others, a really needy one may suffer because the giver has split his donations thinly among a dubious assortment of quasi-charitable drives.

Some insist that the child who participates in fund-raising projects is learning good citizenship, and picks up poise by "meeting the public" at an early age. Balderdash. I doubt if the public appreciates being strong-armed by soft hands so someone else's child may acquire poise.

I dare say that children can acquire considerably more poise in their own homes than they can in the homes of neighbors and strangers.

I think that the good effects of ankle-sock salesmanship are outweighed by the bad. Most adults don't like to ask for money, so picture the emotional distress of the inexperienced, sometimes bumbling child, who's often propelled by pressures from adult "captains" or motivated by an unwholesome competition.

There are some who contend that in these projects the child comes to grips with the plight of the needy and the goodness of giving. I don't think so, because usually the child isn't properly versed on the cause, and in many cases the beneficiary isn't mentioned during the hurried interview.

The whole thing frequently degenerates into a crude pitch wherein the child is forced to say: "Here's what you can win if you buy enough tickets, and here's what I can win if I sell enough."

This is roughly the way it has been and is now in the Chicago area. I like the system in Los Angeles. It's simple and direct: No solicitation of any kind or for any cause by children.

Mrs. Evelyn Spaulding, general manager of that city's Department of Social Service, tells me that the Los Angeles ordinance goes further in the matter of cookies and candy: At least half the price must go to the solicitation agency.

"I must say," she adds, "that the manufacturer does quite well."

As one who has often tasted the stuff, I'd say that the manufacturer does very well.

•••••••••••••••••••••

So the vacation is over. And now—depression.

Not because you must return to work, but because of a guilty conscience. Whatever happened to those fine, noble things you resolved to do while away from the job?

This year, I started my vacation with four goals in sight. I would 1) make a long-threatened switch to a crew cut; 2) read at least three books; 3) learn to float (I'm one of those unfortunate "sinkers" who drop to the bottom of the pool like a stone); and 4) cut down on cigarettes. The results:

1. In the barber's chair I suddenly thought of the pile of bottles of 49-cent hair lotion I've accumulated as Christmas and Father's Day gifts from the little ones. It seemed a shame to let all that greasy kid stuff go to waste. "The usual," I told the barber.

2. I read exactly one book on my vacation, but I read it forty-two times—twice each night for three weeks. The title: *The Brave Little Caboose*. The youngsters roundly applauded each reading.

3. In the pool, I practiced and practiced—to a point where

I must have the world's most chlorinated stomach. I didn't learn to float. But I sink more slowly now.

4. On cigarettes, I cut down from one pack a day to half a pack, replacing the urge with licorice (the only candy I like). It's a great, healthy feeling. One day I took a deep, fresh breath and heard one lung say to the other: "See? That's the stuff I was telling you about." The only thing is, my teeth turned black.

But it wasn't a hopeless hiatus, for I did accomplish one thing of social importance. I put behind me pride, embarrassment, and revulsion and took a significant step.

I stepped into a pair of Bermuda shorts. Not only that, I wore them in public.

You must believe me when I say that it wasn't easy. For years I have been literally revolted by the sight of full-grown males with hairy, lumpy, misshapen legs cavorting about in halfway pantaloons.

It isn't a matter of modesty. It's just that bare knock-knees somehow seem to offend the public gaze. And that goes for men who walk with their legs in parentheses, too.

Never, I vowed. Swim trunks at the beach, fine. Bermuda shorts on the street, not me. And when I make up my mind, I–

What happened, see, is that my wife talked me into taking up tennis ("It's a *young* man's game") and the nude-kneed sports we played with, *they* talked me into shorts.

The shorts arrived, and that night I locked the doors, drew the drapes, and tried them on. Loden green they were, cut an inch above the knees.

"Shouldn't they be longer?" I wondered, hoping they could be returned.

"No," chirped Nelda, "that's the style now–above the knees."

Marcia gasped. "You look adorable," she said.

That did it. "I don't want to look adorable!" I shouted to my wife. "Take them back." But then I thought of the hot hours on the tennis court.

Happily, the next day brought a cold wave, and I won a reprieve. But the day after that was warm, and I had to make my debut in public. I decided to take it in easy stages. In the morning, I dashed to the mailbox and back. Mercifully, nobody saw me. In the afternoon I strolled into the street to retrieve a tricycle. Nobody whistled.

Suddenly that night there came on me a mad craving to smoke, and I was out of licorice. The need was so powerful I totally forgot about my attire, jumped into the car and sped to the store. Then the horror of it all struck me—standing there at the counter in front of others and giving the man a nickel and asking for five licorice sticks, and feeling quite undressed.

If you can go through that, you can go through anything. After that, it was easy.

••••••••••••••••••••••

I thought I was a fair housekeeper, but I'll never broil a pair of sneakers again.

My wife spent a week in Canada visiting her mother, and I took over the eight-head herd. I've done this before, so I'll skip the routine of dusting and cooking and changing diapers. What gets a man down is the extracurricular stuff—and when there are eight youngsters involved, that's a lot of curricular.

Like when little Mark soaked his sneakers playing with the water hose. The sun would take too long to dry them out, so why not pop them into the oven? I was heating up the oven anyway for a covey of chicken potpies, and everything was going fine until Lisa accidentally broke a neighbor's window.

I was having a devil of a time removing the splintered glass when Shonagh walked up and asked what we were having for dinner. I said chicken potpie. She said it sure didn't smell like chicken potpie in the kitchen. I almost severed an artery getting back to the oven and the two miserable clumps of shriveled canvas.

Over chicken that night—a little gamy, mind you, but all right—it struck me that most men forget that unexpected, irregular things keep happening at home during their absence. After the homemaker has the dishes done and the beds made, serenity doesn't necessarily follow. For example:

We all trooped off to the supermarket (have you ever tried to get TWO babies into the cart?) and among the things they talked me into buying was a pair of goldfish—Flame and Blackie (now I have twelve mouths to feed). It took some talking to convince the smaller ones that Flame and Blackie wouldn't be comfortable in the back-yard wading pool. I told them I didn't want to start any new trends in the suburb.

The next day, as I was changing the fish water, Flame slipped out of my hand and to the floor, and as I was trying to retrieve the frightened, squirming thing, Barbara ran in to announce that she was in immediate need of answering one of nature's calls, and just then the telephone rang. I decided that Flame, near death on the floor, was more important at the moment and consequently Barbara answered nature's call in her own, primitive way—perilously close to Flame. I did, however, save the fish.

The housekeeper must also make decisions as to whose turn it is to have a little friend stay overnight. One night I had three youngsters sleeping with my own, and Lisa, who felt left out, wanted HER friend (a boy) to share her bed. "There's no room left!" I yelled. "They're sleeping on the floor now!"

"Me and Larry can sleep in the car," she suggested.

The recent night of the eclipse I let all but Mark and Barbara stay out to watch the phenomenon, while I sorted the ankle socks from out the dryer. (Good grief, they're all the same length, aren't they?) Suddenly, Nelda rushed in and asked: "Is Mark and Barbara safe in bed?" I said they were.

"Good!" she said. "Because the moon's coming down—*right now!*" With that she ran out again to watch the disaster.

The housekeeper must also be a chauffeur: Each afternoon I had to drive Paul to his job at a nearby restaurant (where he's the sanitation engineer) and fetch him back each night. I took them to see a movie and to pool parties around the neighborhood and to the dentist and hither and yon and back again, and now I know what my wife's doing out there in the hot neighborhood while I sit in this air-conditioned office.

Apart from the broken window there were no disasters except that a mosquito bit me on the eyelid. This makes the lid droop down over the eye so that you look pretty decrepit. The result was that several neighbors would walk up and leer: "Having yourself a time while your wife's away, aren't you?"

But everything turned out well. And thank heaven for the hamburger drive-in.

••••••••••••••••••••••

I was at the supermarket the other day, having a devil of a time in the cereal section. You know how it is in that department, with something like ninety brands of breakfast food all wedged so tightly that when you pluck one box the whole shebang comes toppling down.

I was up to my knees in snap-crackle-and-pop, when a friendly clerk came over to help. "I want one atomic submarine," I said, "and one magic aquarium."

"Atomic submarine?" he asked.

"Yes," I said. "The one that really dives."

He pursed his lips and looked around, as if for help. "And a magic aquarium?"

"Yes," I said, "the one with the fish and turtle that really swim."

It took a little explaining but I finally got through to the young man. Nowadays, you don't identify a breakfast cereal by its name on the front of the box—most of the weird names all sound alike anyway—but by the information on the back of the box.

So I got what the two youngest of the youngsters had requested—the cereal with the atomic sub that really dives (free, in the box), and the cereal with the magic aquarium and plastic fish and turtle that really swim (this one you get later by sending in fifty cents and a box top).

While there, I looked at other cereals, and now I know why the clothes closet at home is crammed with box tops, coupons, and empty piggy banks. The gimmicks those food folks use to get at the children's allowance!

Here's one that offers them a genuine bowling game for one dollar and two box tops. Here's a "flying platform" for only a quarter and one top. For the same tariff you can send for a set of horseshoes and ring toss, or a set of "crazy calling cards" (whatever those are), or—are you ready for Mother's Day?—four plastic juice glasses.

For fifty cents and one top you can get an "educational" zoo, seven animals ready for assembling, or a miniature golf game. Seventy-five cents and one top bring you a Halloween costume; the same amount, with three tops, is worth a birdhouse and feeder kit (made of redwood).

(Since this is January, that Halloween offer made me wonder just how fresh the cereal really is, or are they rushing next October a little?)

For a dollar, plus a top, you can send for various games like building sets, cargo ships, and so on. For the same price, Mother is promised a five-piece scissors set or a bow-maker kit. For two dollars, there are assorted sets of silverware, and if you care to part with five dollars you can acquire a label maker.

Not all of the items cost money, though. Some cereals have crossword puzzles, comic books, and cowboy figurines on the inside or outside. One box has a taffy bar inside. Great thing, taffy, to start breakfast with.

One cereal whose maker I don't intend to patronize asks the kids to cough up $12.88 for a three-foot army tank (minus batteries), or a doll that "tells you how she feels when you push the button." She also coughs and sneezes. At that price, I'll send for her when she can wash dishes and mop the floor.

A little later, I spoke with the store manager. "You often hear the parents and kids arguing about the prizes in the box," he said, "or what they can get for box tops. It's a little sad. And besides, this whole business messes up my shelves."

He should see the messes these gimmicks create at home.

Let's see, now, where do they keep the pancake flour?

••••••••••••••••••••••

It all started innocently enough, with an outlay of $2.00.

After weeks of mounting pressure, I have given in to the children's demands for a pair of rabbits. Bringing such prolific creatures to the Molloy eight-youngster household is somewhat like carrying coals to Newcastle, and I found the idea less than entrancing. But the children, who have been reading the papers, adopted tactics that were hard to overcome.

They engaged in sit-ins, lay-ins, pray-ins, cry-ins, and similar demonstrations. They left petitions in what I laughingly call my study (the room that houses the laundry hamper, the ironing board, the record player, the vacuum cleaner, and sundry other household items).

When they took to flinging themselves prone at the bathroom intersection, halting all important traffic, I capitulated.

After all, it would only be a couple of dollars for the bunnies, and carrots are cheap, and I'd build a little hutch and—

It didn't turn out quite like that. My talent with a hammer and saw is woeful, and when I got through demolishing the two orange crates I couldn't have given the mess away as toothpicks. I called in a carpenter.

That was the first blow. He was booked weeks ahead but he would come in on this "special"—at $10 an hour, and the pay started from the first hello on the telephone (the other carpenters in the area had the same little racket worked up among them).

I called the carpenter at eight o'clock in the morning. He arrived at eight-thirty, and I'd already spent $5.00 before we'd even drawn the first sketch. Planning the architecture and collecting the supplies took us to ten o'clock, by which time I'd spent $20 on the carpenter, $28 for lumber and $10 for mesh, staples, screws, a lock, and paint and brush.

Fortunately the carpenter had come equipped with nails, but $58 had flown away, and not a nail had been hammered.

A rabbit hutch, or warren, I discovered, is like nothing else in the world. You must allow for southern exposure and erect a wooden side to fend off the north winds and build a bed (with straw) and talc the openings and slant the roof against the rain and install a pull-out tray at the bottom, because rabbits have a rather active digestive process.

As I watched it going up on small stilts (how else do you dispose of their bowel movements?), it seemed to have everything except a two-car garage and air conditioning. Unable to bear it, I departed to spend more money.

You don't feed carrots to bunnies except as an occasional treat (if they get hooked on carrots they'll reject the ordinary fare). They need "pellets," the complete food. And two heavy bowls, for water and pellets, that won't tip over when they play tag—and I get the impression they play tag all day and far into the night. And you need straw. And shavings for the tray. And a salt disk for hot weather. And so on.

To save a little, I painted the hutch myself. I painted it red, neatly matching the sunburn I got wielding the brush in 90-plus heat. It got so hot at one point that I broke out a couple of soft drinks, and the carpenter and I sat in the shade to relax. It was only when I drained the last gulp that I realized we'd blown a half-hour. That recess had cost me another $5.00—$5.20 if you count the two drinks.

While the paint was drying overnight the bunnies slept in a carton box in what we call the Vaster Bedroom, the one that houses Nelda, Marcia, Lisa, Barbara, and Mark. The five didn't sleep much that night, because the long-eared pair kept hopping out and leaving evidence of their exploring all over the floor and in the children's slippers and in Mark's dump truck.

We call the black-and-white one Fibber. The blond one, who resembles Peter O'Toole, answers to Molly. I figure the McGees have cost me, so far, well over $100. I'll never recoup unless they click conjugally and we resign ourselves to eating rabbit all winter.

But there is no certainty in that. They're six weeks old. We know that Molly is a little girl, but because of nature's mischievous ways we cannot be certain for a little while yet that Fibber is a little boy. Male rabbits have a way of concealing their sex that is a bit complicated to describe in a family newspaper. He—uh, it will let us know around the first of September.

Somehow I have the uneasy feeling that we're on the verge of a population explosion.

••••••••••••••••••••••

If you're male, married, and full of yourself—turn to the comic strips. This is not for you.

I just found out what my wife is worth.

Not down to the last dollar, maybe, but close enough to set me thinking. And if you're male, married, and full of yourself—and you're still here—it may set you thinking too.

In a weak moment the other night I told my wife I'd do the dishes. Estimating five minutes each for the mess left by eight children and two adults, I figured I'd have the job done in less than an hour. It took me two hours and twenty-three minutes. I'd forgotten that there's more to washing dishes than washing dishes.

There's making the little ones finish their meal, and retrieving the crusts hidden behind saucers, and washing the rainbows of ketchup and cocoa off the toddlers' faces, and sweeping two floors (kitchen and dinette), and washing the counter tops and stove, and emptying the garbage (two trips), and doing the silverware and glasses separately, and putting away the leftovers (and pausing to change a diaper), and making the next day's school lunches.

Bless my detergent hands, I just know there'll be mail saying I could solve the problem with a dishwasher. Not so. You can't make a lunch or change a diaper with a dishwasher. Besides, I figured it out that if I could squeeze a dishwasher into our pre-fab, the stove and two children would have to go. And we need the stove.

Anyway, the whole business got me thinking about a home economics report from Cornell University that I read and tucked away last winter. (Don't ask me why I collect these things. With some people it's stamps, or blondes. With me—it's home economics reports.)

This study sets down the value of the homemaker's services by applying current wage rates to the average work loads. I tell you, this is going to hurt—but the work-and-wages chart is a thing of detailed, scientific beauty. For example, meal preparation ($1.83 an hour) is divided into meals with only quick foods (fifteen minutes), meals with one time-consuming dish (thirty minutes), and meals with four or more time-consuming dishes (sixty minutes). For ten people at my house, I figured it down to $31.99 a week.

The chart says that dishwashing (the whole cycle from table to cleaning the sink, counters, and range) should take one hour and thirty minutes for a family of five at $1.22 an hour. If I hired someone for this job, then, it would cost me $33.88 a week. Ironing would cost me $6.10 a week and clothes washing (we average three tubfuls a day) would come to $14.64.

Under child care, the chart says I should include physical care, homework help, and chauffeuring—but NOT playing with them or supervising them. That would come to $14 a week. Routine housecleaning (not including big, seasonal projects) would set me back $100.65 a week.

This is the general stuff. I listed nothing under shopping for food, caring for the sick, gardening, buying clothes, moving furniture, changing the ribbon in my typewriter, and so on. For ordinary services, however, my wife earns—but doesn't get—$10,465.52 a year.

There are other things for which it's hard to set a price—love, comfort, the thrill of having a beautiful date whenever I feel like it, her setting an example for the children, her reading my column, her fighting nine different kinds of flu—I've counted none of this.

And already I owe my wife $10,465.52 a year.

As I say—it sets you to thinking, doesn't it?

•••••••••••••••••••••

It happened Christmas Eve.

We had left the four smaller children at home in the care of a sitter, and the older three—Paul, Georgia, and Shonagh—were coming with us to Midnight Mass.

In my own boyhood the custom of Midnight Mass was one to be savored for life: The rare thrill of rising from bed in the crisp darkness of 11 P.M. . . . our shadows in the snowbank nagging us to step up the pace . . . the resin smell of spruce cones from the outdoor crèche in the churchyard . . . the muffled, giggly greetings in the vestibule . . . and from within the wheezy bravado of the little organ bluffing through "Adeste Fidelis."

So it was that Helen, cautious now with the weight of the eighth child we expected later, led the three youngsters into the pew, and I tried to remember where on earth I had hidden Nelda's top—the one with the ballerina pirouetting out of the burgeoning rose. And throughout the Mass the children swayed between prayer and distraction, and the glow no words can touch was all around.

And then the priest was in the pulpit and we stood and he introduced the Gospel of St. Luke, and suddenly I remembered that the top was inside the tub hanging in the utility room. And out of the candled blur up front droned the voice of the priest:

"*. . . and it came to pass while they were there that the days for her to be delivered were fulfilled. And she brought forth . . .*"

And when we sat again I felt the sudden nudge of Helen's elbow, and I turned to find in her eyes a flicker of concern. She glanced sideways. She whispered: "I think we have to go."

"Go?" I said, much too loud. She leaned over again: "I think it's time." And then her face winced in a silent stab of pain. "Now!" she said.

Oh no, I thought, recalling the sometimes suddenness of these things. And as I gathered up the mittens and scarves I felt the cold clasp of panic—let no man say he gets used to these things—and for one ghastly moment a qualm buckled my knees: The baby's coming now, I thought, right in this church—right by the manger.

But we had a little time and this subdued the panic. It was, however, a long, slow walk down the middle aisle. And as we hustled into the tired little car—as much as we could hustle under the conditions—Paul (then twelve) leaned over and said: "The thing to do, Dad, is not to get excited."

We scudded home to drive the three, and as I drove to the hospital the thought swirled through my head: Here it is, the monumental explosion of Christmas, and we've been expecting a fat stranger with round cheeks and twinkling eyes, but this—

And at three o'clock that Christmas morning, Mark was born, and after we talked awhile Helen mumbled: "He's beautiful . . . but how will you manage the turkey and everything?" And I got home before the others awoke and placed the gifts beneath the tree, and then the first Christmas yell wahooed from one of the bedrooms, and the shouting seven bounded into the living room, and the fandango was on. And then I told them what had happened during the night of the Christ Child's birthday. I must have been tired, because my voice seemed to crack a little.

"Let's call him Jesus!" cried Nelda. "Jesus Molloy."

"No, we're going to call him Mark," I said.

"I think Jesus is gooder," said Nelda.

Marcia reached down. "Look at the pretty top," she shrilled.

It's funny how you remember little things in moments of emotion.

It was quite a night, and quite a day.

And I'll never have to go very far for a Christmas story.

I'm just standing there, waiting for a cab...

There's a little bit of good even in the troublesome things, and the current taxicab strike in Chicago is a good example.

I suspect the strike has brought some relief to those riders who have a twinge of conscience when boarding a hack for a short run. The twinge is there because they know deep down they're pampering themselves and should be taking a bus—or even walking.

I refer especially to commuters who have but a brief hop from the railway stations to their offices in the Loop. They could make it in just minutes on the bus, but there's something about an empty cab at the curb that gets them (me included).

You know how it is. You make up reasons for taking a taxi. The bus may be delayed somewhere. If the bus is there it looks too crowded. If it's not crowded you suddenly remember there's pressing business at the office and you should be there quickly—like now.

And of course you get there quickly and spend forty minutes sipping coffee and gazing out the window and bothering other workers at their desks.

So the habit is formed and guilt creeps in, but there's always a good excuse. Hasn't the back been acting up lately? Better take a cab. You're depressed, so take a cab. You had an argument with your wife and the breakfast toast was burned, so take a cab. You're worried about that raise that hasn't come through yet, so take a cab. There's an important article in the paper that you want to read in private comfort, so take a cab. You've got some deep, deep thinking to do about an important decision, so take a cab because you can't concentrate on a bus with all those peasants coughing.

Now you know you're really hooked, so this morning you'll pass up the taxi. But a friend invites you to be his guest in his taxi, and what happens? Next morning you emerge from the station together and of course you must return the courtesy so you ask him to be YOUR guest this time. This Alphonse-Gaston routine can be murder on the pocketbook.

And so it goes, and you know you shouldn't be blowing that money when it isn't really necessary, and the more you ride around the more guilty you become. Until you promise yourself that you'll kick the habit any day now. In fact, you'll kick it tomorrow.

So tomorrow comes, and it's raining and you've just had your suit pressed. Take a cab. You'll kick the habit the next day.

Next day comes and you're carrying parcels. Too bulky for the bus. Take a cab and tomorrow—for sure—you'll line up for the bus.

And tomorrow you remember that the night before you won $27.50 at the poker game. You can afford a cab one more morning . . .

The fact is you just don't want to admit that you're lazy and you exult in the luxury of being chauffeured to work. You're trapped, like an alcoholic, and you wish there were something called Cab Riders Anonymous.

Then comes the strike, and there are no longer six taxis

waiting for you at the curb. Now you're back on the bus again, and it isn't too bad. You'd forgotten how comfortable and fairly swift the bus is.

That's it. You've got the monkey off your back. No more cabs for that short trip. This is the way it should be. And this is the way it's going to be when this strike is over, too, by golly.

Hmmmm . . .

•••••••••••••••••••••

That government report on smoking wasn't all bad. Now that a week has gone by, the smokers and the abstainers have had time to line up—to ponder or to boast.

If you're a people-watcher, you'll gain some new insights into human behavior by observing the gang at the plant or office. Chances are you'll find one or more of the following specimens:

Clarence Cleanbill: Probably the world's most exasperating bore. He has never smoked in his life, and not a day goes by but he tells you about his astounding self-control (all the while fanning away your smoke with his hands). Ask him how he avoided the filthy habit, and he'll say: "I never needed it." Small wonder. He drinks like a fish.

Stanley Stoutfellow: Some time ago he read that substitution was the best way to kick the habit. He decided on chocolate bars. He now weighs 283 pounds, and high blood pressure will land him on the obituary page in six months.

Sherman Shakespine: That report scared him out of his wits, making him so nervous he's now on four packs a day.

Chester Chindrool: This fellow went into absolute ecstasy when the report made no mention of chewing tobacco. But don't bump into him on a crowded bus.

Dudley Deadbeat: He swore off in 1959, but didn't really quit smoking. He merely switched brands—to OP's (Other People's). Enterprising fellow. With the money he saved he put a son through college and installed a handsome patio in the back yard.

Claudia Clockwatcher: Her solution is to limit herself to one cigarette an hour. At twenty minutes to the hour she's sucking her thumb, tugging at her girdle, linking paper clips, and snapping at everyone in sight. By July she'll have clean lungs and a nervous breakdown.

Bobby Beaubrummel: He feels safe because he affects a long cigarette holder, from whose end he spends much time extracting the butts. There's no cancer in his lungs. It's in his fingernails.

Cyril Cirrhosis: No problem. He joined Smokers Anonymous. Whenever a member gets that uncontrollable urge to light up, he calls up a friend who rushes over, and the two of them get stoned.

Arthur Artifice: He told his wife he was through with gaspers, but at the office he smokes up a smog. All the way home he chews gum, lozenges, and licorice. His wife keeps wondering why he insists on walking the dog at 9 P.M., 10 P.M., 11 P.M., midnight, and first thing in the morning at a quarter to 6.

Belvedere Belch: Years ago he learned to curb the need by downing a bottle of soda pop. His carbonated kidney not only floats, it does the Australian crawl.

Roscoe Restraint: This specimen guards his health by pacing himself—one puff and he puts down the cigarette anywhere that's handy. In his time he's burned down two homes, a night club, his insurance adjuster's office, and sixteen desks. If he comes to your house, cover up the mahogany.

Nick O'Tean: Belongs to the you-only-live-once school, a cigarette always dangling from his lips. Hasn't had a speck of trouble—since that left lung came out. And the teeth. And the bladder.

Everett Everglow: Serene type. Discovered tranquilizers years ago and doesn't have a care in the world. Still writes 1964 on his checks and letters.

Gregory Greyflannel: Sad case. Brilliant creator of cigarette commercials. Thought up the lines, "It's what's up front that counts," "And they are mild," etc. Earned $80,000 a year. Got pink-slipped the day the report came out. Has tattoo, will travel.

Fortescue Fourscore: There's one of these in every crowd. Started on cornsilk at five, smoked cigarettes, pipe, and hookah, and died at ninety-three when he slipped on the dance floor, doing the frug.

●●●●●●●●●●●●●●●●●●●●●

I keep wondering if we aren't about to noise ourselves to death.

Almost everywhere you go nowadays music seems to be seeping out of the walls or the ceiling or the floor. And in some cases I'm not at all sure that music is the right word.

I'm one of those old-fashioned cusses who likes a little peace and quiet. Not all the time, mind you—I'm not greedy. But just three or four times a day I want to be without the fox trots and frugs and waltzes that keep banging at me from all sides.

You're sitting in the doctor's office, telling him about your bad back or something, and suddenly Mantovani comes out of the X-ray machine or the instrument cabinet with "Get Me to the Church on Time." And did you ever have a cavity filled to the tune of the Grand Canyon Suite? I have. Ghastly.

I'm not knocking music, but it's so incessant and everywhere and all the time. And don't tell me about the wake-up-to-music radios; I'm four-square against them. (Can you imagine what waking up to Phil Harris' "Ding Dong Daddy from Paducah" can do to your day?)

You strap yourself into a plane seat and out of the ceiling comes "Danse Macabre." You step into the elevator and out of the ceiling comes Jane Morgan and "Fascination" (I'm convinced Miss Morgan has agents all around the country who play "Fascination" every hour on the hour). You pinch the tomatoes in the supermarket and out of the ceiling comes "Never on Sunday." You sit in the restaurant and out of the ceiling comes the theme from *Exodus*. You flee to the men's room to escape it all and out of the ceiling comes the theme from *Spartacus*.

For some people, this isn't enough. In case they're caught some place where there's no ceiling (like at the beach), or some place where the ceiling won't co-operate (like on commuter trains), they carry a transistor radio to their ear.

(I don't know what it is with me on commuter trains, but I have ruddy bad luck most of the time. I get settled, open the newspaper, and the moment the train pulls out the fellow next to me pulls out his transistor and leans back, grinning like a cat. If I don't get him, I get the lady who frowns on smoking. There'll be eight no-smoking coaches on the train and one smoker. And darned if the anti-nicotines don't pick the smoker and head for my seat just as I'm pulling out a gasper.)

But about those transistor radios: I think it's frightful how they're taking over the country. You see people venturing into traffic, heads tilted to the left and right, elbows up in the air and oblivious to life around them. Just last week I ran into a middle-aged lady with cauliflower ears; don't tell me transistors aren't dangerous.

And they have strange effects too. I've always liked baseball and I leaned to the Chicago White Sox, and my idea of ecstasy is an afternoon at the ball park, fairly close to home plate.

But invariably I've been sitting near characters who bring their transistors to the park. I mean the kind who weren't content to watch one game on the field and let it go at that. They had to tune in the Chicago Cubs playing somewhere on the road. For two years I've been listening to the Cubs while watching the Sox.

And that's how I became a Cubs fan.

••••••••••••••••••••

Anyone care to join my new club? I call it SAPS Inc., and I can use some members. Its aim is to destroy a national sickness.

SAPS stands for Society for the Abolition of Palm-Slappers—that tribe of hand-happy imbeciles who clap and yell at the wrong times. Their specialty is ruining the start and close of an act. They are the spoilers who infest theaters, night clubs, and now television studios.

The moment that Maurice Chevalier starts the first notes of "Louise," the hand-clappers spring into action and drown it out. I hear Chevalier does well with "Louise," but I've never heard much beyond: "Every little breeze seems to whisper clap-clap." When the late Sophie Tucker was on the night-club floor, dozens of dolts would shriek: "Give us 'Some of These Days,' Sophie!" And she would: "Some of these days, you're gonna clap-clap-clap-clap."

In Hollywood recently, a friend took me to the Cocoanut

Grove to see Gordon MacRae's act. Everybody bellowed for him to render "Oklahoma!" with which he's long been associated. MacRae obliged but got only as far as "OK–" (without the exclamation point, yet). That was the signal for six hundred retarded patty-cakers.

Has anyone ever heard Judy Garland sing her theme? The boors in the audience have consistently forced her to settle for "Somewhere over the clap-clap." A few weeks ago I was close enough to Hildegarde to smell the perfume on her kerchief, but when she did her trade-mark all I got was "Darling, je vous clap-clap-clap." And I've become resigned to the fact that Ted Lewis' sign-off is "When My Baby Smiles clap-clap," followed by the traditional: "Is Everybody clap-clap?"

An old-timer of my acquaintance who happens to be a Gracie Fields fan still believes her wartime classic was "Wish Me Luck As You Wave Me clap-clap." And my dad used to tell me he had seen three of Harry Lauder's farewell performances, and each time it came out "Roamin' in the clap-clap."

This has been going on since the days of big-time radio. I've always enjoyed Kate Smith, especially when she came across with "When the Moon Comes Over the clap-clap." Nor can I think of Nelson Eddy without thinking of the memorable "Mammy's li'l baby loves clap-clap, clap-clap." And who will ever forget Carol Channing belting out her lilting "Hello, clap-clap?"

Some experienced hands among the premature sound-offs are so adept that they can actually drown out the introduction of the speaker's name at a civic meeting. After I'd finished a talk on a recent night a nice lady in the audience came up to the rostrum, shook my hand vigorously and said: "Thank you for a most inspiring address, Mr. clap-clap."

In any event, it's time for an organization like SAPS Inc. Christmas isn't too far away and THIS time, by golly, my youngsters want to hear Perry Como do that cute little Yule melody—how does it go again? . . . Oh yes, "Rudolph, the clap-Nosed clap-clap."

••••••••••••••••••••••

There's been much talk lately of what happiness really is. Happiness is a warm puppy. Happiness is the car starting in twelve below zero. Happiness is winding up with a tax refund, and so on. But what about frustration? What is it?

Frustration, in church, is when the collection plate comes around and the smallest thing you have is a $20 bill.

Frustration is getting Christmas cards on December 26 from nine people who weren't on your list.

Frustration, on the way to work, is looking down at your feet to find the socks don't match.

Frustration is warm toast and frozen butter.

Frustration, at a wedding reception, is when the photographer snaps your picture just as you're putting a forkful of angel cake in your mouth.

Frustration is taking a half-hour to lace on the children's skates, then finding them back at the door two minutes later with a mad desire for the bathroom.

Frustration is a long-distance call when you're standing in the shower.

Frustration is coming upon a car astride two parking places.

Frustration is when the string of lights blows out on the Christmas tree after the stores are closed for the weekend.

Frustration is thumbing through a dictionary, then realizing you've forgotten the word you were looking for.

Frustration is when the television repairman says he can't get to your house for another ten days.

Frustration is waiting in line for a railway ticket.

Frustration is being asked to take a bow at a public function just as a massive, lung-collapsing cough shakes you asunder.

Frustration is getting a statement from the dentist that says "Please!"

Frustration is the gas-station attendant who can't get your hood opened, then smears your windshield with a used tissue.

Frustration is receiving a gift with the sender's card missing.

Frustration is asking a casual acquaintance how the wife and kids are, and having him remind you he's a bachelor.

Frustration is never remembering the size of your wife's hosiery.

Frustration, in the supermarket, is racing two women to the check-out counter—and losing.

Frustration is the secretary who says: "Mr. Smith is calling—will you hold the line?"

Frustration, at the bank, is waiting in line twenty minutes when you haven't noticed that the fellow in front of you is a storekeeper with a week's deposits.

Frustration is when the waiter breathes down your neck all through dinner and, when it's time to leave, is nowhere to be found.

Frustration is looking at ten toothbrushes in the bathroom, and forgetting which one is your color.

Frustration is discovering, after a long wait, that you never did plug in the coffeepot.

Frustration is the dog down the street that has taken an unaccountable liking to your lawn.

Frustration is a slow elevator in a forty-story building.

Frustration, if you're a columnist, is having someone say he reads you every day—in another newspaper.

••••••••••••••••••••

Has anyone else noticed? You mention to friends that you're taking a trip and three out of four will ask if you're going by plane. If the answer is no, more often than not they'll give you a strange stare (made stranger when it comes from folks who themselves have never been aloft).

Sometimes the situation calls for this rejoinder: "Flying is against my religion—I'm a devout coward." But this is a lame offering when cowardice isn't involved.

In my own case, I don't lack confidence in planes. Heights don't bother me and I actually enjoy takeoffs and landings, which are supposed to be unnerving. I've flown alone with bush pilots over the northern Canadian wilds, and in sleek airliners, and my only distress has been a case of claustrophobia. When the plane door slams shut, I feel a bit trapped, because I like elbow room. I get the same feeling in those high-rise push-button elevators.

But this isn't enough to keep a man off planes, and I'll use them if I'm in a real hurry. The thing is, I've grown sick and tired of being in a ceaseless, stupid, rush-rush hurry. What does it get you? Short breath and high blood pressure.

So I fell in love with trains a few years ago, and I guess the reason is simply that trains are fun. I refer especially to the all-bedroom trains on long runs such as the Pennsylvania's Broadway Limited to New York or the Santa Fe's Super Chief to California.

I figure a trip like that, with excellent dining and sleeping accommodations, is fine therapy for anyone with a harried working schedule. It's like taking a miniature vacation—getting away for a night or two from the hustle and bustle of the daily grind.

One thing I like about trains (maybe as a child I wanted to be an engineer) is that it departs when it's supposed to depart and arrives (in most cases) on schedule—and only a few minutes from the hotel. I also know that bad weather won't shunt me off to another city.

But best of all—no claustrophobia. If a cramped feeling does come over you, you can shake it by walking up and down the length of the train, and there's always the thought that if you've had it, you can leave it all behind and get off at the next stop and stay there for a while. I get off at most stops, even if it's midnight. Childish, perhaps, but I get a charge out of it.

I'm not especially gregarious, so I generally find the lounge car a bore. My idea of real relaxation, real unwinding, is to sit in the privacy of the compartment with a couple dollars' worth of magazines and a book or two I've been wanting to read. And looking out the window—even into the black nothingness of night. For it's good for one to be alone once in a while—to think, meditate, and yes, even loaf.

And I can't think of a better place to do it than on the train, especially when you're but a minute away from the dining car. I don't know what it is, but a steak seems to taste ever so much better when you're rolling through the countryside.

I guess I'm hooked on trains, and perhaps riding them has become a hobby. But I do wish the railroads would speed up and streamline their ticket-selling system. It's outmoded and primitive.

Apart from that I have a love affair with trains. And now, when people ask why I'm not flying I smile to myself and hear again the wailing blast of the engine up front. I think it's romantic.

••••••••••••••••••••••

There is an ailment abroad in the land which, for want of a name, could be called melodylingersonitis.

It's a sort of mental quirk whereby the mind latches on to a melody or snatch of song and can't get rid of it. I've got it bad and I wonder how many others have the affliction.

It's an irritating thing and appears more prevalent during the warm-weather season when people have their car windows down and you can't escape the blare of their radios.

With me, at the moment, the problem is "Supercalifragilisticexpialidocious." This one is from the *Mary Poppins* movie and it has been running around on the top of my head, somewhere, for three weeks. I can't count the hours of sleep that "Supercalifragilisticexpialidocious" has robbed me of.

If you haven't awakened at two o'clock in the morning humming "Supercalifragilisticexpialidocious" and not been able to chase it away, and have it happen again at three o'clock, and then at four o'clock, you simply haven't suffered.

A little earlier this year it was a monotonous ditty called "Downtown" which was particularly oppressive because I don't happen to like the words.

There is no way of telling what melody will hit you, or when. Sometimes you'll be free of symptoms for a couple of months and you think you've licked it when it suddenly reappears with a song you've not heard for perhaps fifteen years.

At Christmastime, when everyone else was going around humming "White Christmas," I was stuck—night and day—with "The Prisoner's Song," a weepy lament I hadn't heard in a quarter of a century.

Last year I got caught by the "Double Your Pleasure" gum-commercial lyric and that one stayed with me from May through September. I tried to shoo it away by fighting fire with fire—humming other melodies like "Danse Macabre" and "Redheads on Parade" but it was no use. As much as I'd try to control it I'd eventually segue into "Double Your Pleasure" (Try singing to yourself the words of "Double Your Pleasure" to the tune of "Danse Macabre" and you'll know what I mean).

Others I've had trouble with include "Monkey on a String"; "On the Beach at Waikiki" and Beethoven's Symphony No. 4, in B Flat Major, Opus 60. And whenever I hear "Hello, Dolly" I just take off and hide somewhere.

This situation reached an appalling climax one afternoon when, waiting for a light change at an intersection, I found myself not only humming one of these nagging things, but singing it out loud to myself in the car. A lady stopped her car alongside of mine and I was suddenly aware that she was giving me the oddest stare.

I don't blame her. Imagine a full-grown man staring into space and singing:

I'd love to be an Oscar Mayer wiener,
That is what I'd truly like to be-ee-ee;
For if I was an Oscar Mayer wiener,
Everyone would be in love with me-ee-ee.

Funny thing, though. At the next intersection the lady and I were car-mates again. And darned if she wasn't humming the wiener aria. This time there was no odd stare. I had recognized a fellow-sufferer. And she knew I understood . . .

●●●●●●●●●●●●●●●●●●●●

I've just come back from lunch with another telephony. It's always an unnerving experience.

The telephony is the insecure boor who gets the vapors if he's more than four yards away from a phone. The moment he's seated in the restaurant he calls for a phone and starts dialing like crazy. Between calls he'll look up at you and say, in a voice that carries to at least five adjoining tables: "Be right with you—soon as I put in this call to Otto."

While you sit there, wondering if it's Otto Kerner, the governor, or Otto Preminger, the movie producer, this fraud is calling his tailor—Otto Cummerbund—about a long-overdue bill.

Most telephonies are in or around show business, though their numbers sometimes include career women, unsuccessful lawyers, and unemployed politicians. They're usually found in places frequented by celebrities, and the busiest one I ever saw was the one who lunched with two phones going full blast. He was able to do this because his lunch consisted of Metrecal, which he sucked through a straw.

Telephonies are almost always table-hoppers, and that can bring on some shattering involvements. Once I was lunching with one telephony when another paused at the table and asked to borrow the phone. They very nearly came to blows. On another occasion I sat in silence for ten minutes while the telephony across from me gave indication of conversing with a film executive in Hollywood. I couldn't bring myself to tell him that the executive was in a nearby booth trying to annihilate a hangover.

A friend of mine likes to tell about a hambone actor who hasn't had a role in a dozen years. During lunch the actor called a prominent producer in New York, demanded, and got a part in an upcoming play. When it was over he put down the phone and told my friend: "This guy (the producer) is a doll, but you've got to be firm with him." At that point the waiter came along and quietly plugged the extension cord into the wall socket.

Sometimes the telephony will try a little reverse finesse: He gets people to phone *him* at the restaurant. The trouble with this technique is that you can spot it in minutes. The telephony sits there, fretting and glancing at his watch, unable to make conversation, lighting the wrong end of his cigar and drumming the table with his fork. Finally he'll signal the headwaiter and say: "I'm Puff Adder, the press agent. If there's any calls for me I'll be right here." Where else, for goodness sakes?

I believe the ultimate in bad manners is the letter-reading, doodle-scratching telephony. This is the dunderhead who brings his morning mail to lunch, cradles the phone on his shoulder, jabbers to someone in Boston, rips open a pile of envelopes and doodles on the tablecloth. After a long session of this he gets up and says: "It's been fun, baby. Let's have lunch again real soon."

Snubs aside, the telephony presents certain hazards. I understand that during a spaghetti lunch, one time, a waiter ran over to a telephony who was trying to impress people, screamed, "You're turning purple!" and deftly pulled a yard of phone cord from his throat.

You can't do much about the telephony except avoid him. But once I had a beautiful dream. I met a telephony for lunch, ordered a typewriter, and wrote a column as he munched corn on the cob. As he chewed from left to right, see, I typed from right to left.

And every time the little bell rang: POW!!—right in the kisser.

••••••••••••••••••••••

What's with all the kissing lately? I mean in public. Has anybody else noticed?

You arrive at a party, and you're no sooner through the door when—WHUMPP!—the hostess (whose first name you may have forgotten) stamps a scarlet smear all over your cheek. You make your way through the crowd and WHUMPP! WHUMPP! WHUMPP!—now you're getting it left and right. By the time you find a chair, wiping the propylene glycol monostearate (that's what it is, really) off your puss, you look like you're coming down with galloping eczema.

The poor fellow who must attend a couple of cocktail parties weekly has it rough. For the cocktail party seems to be a natural habitat of the predatory kisser. "Baby *doll!*" some female gushes, "haven't seen *you* in simply *ages!*"

This exuberance is followed by one or two WHUMPPS and Baby Doll retreats—but too late. He backs into somebody's soggy hors d'oeuvre, cigarette ash makes a gray snow on his shirt, half an ounce of martini splatters his tie, and there's a sloppy red print near his chin. He's been at this bash just half an hour, mind you, but he gets home looking (and smelling) like fun-and-games, and his wife—well, let's draw the curtain on THAT domestic scene.

For the record, lipstick and other cosmetics have too long a history to be outlawed. When they opened up the royal tomb at Ur, in Babylonia, they found lipstick among the goodies buried with female departees—and that was four thousand years ago. Nero, that insufferable fiddler, wore lipstick, and Elizabeth I, the sixteenth-century "virgin queen," concocted her own in the royal boudoir. Indeed it was quite the thing in those days for the ladies of the realm to whip up their own private batches of beauty aids.

Despite this ancient background, oddly enough, it wasn't until 1915 that lipstick was actually marketed in this country. Before that, only wealthy women had the means and time to indulge in elaborate toilette. What did the poor working girls do? In secret, they rubbed beet juice on their lips and patted wheat flour on their cheeks.

We've come a long way since. Catching up on my reading (*Vogue, Mademoiselle*), I came across full-page Du Barry ads for something called "Glissando," which the maker describes as a "real breakthrough." I gather it's the most smashing thing since Antony looked at Cleopatra's toenails and giggled: "Forsooth, they've turned green!"

This "Glissando," if I read it right, blends a medley of several shades into a single stick. "Imagine," trills the ad, "in every stick of 'Glissando' you see myriad shades swirling into each other, blending with perfect artistry into a luscious cosmetic parfait!" I'm sorry, but all I see is a luscious bloody accident all over my collar. Still, it's an improvement over that little old beet juice.

But some have tried to outlaw the goo and kindred aids. In 1770, a bill was introduced in the British Parliament which provided: "That all women of whatever age, rank or profession that shall impose upon, seduce and betray into matrimony any of His Majesty's subjects by the scents, paints, cosmetic washes, artificial teeth, false hair, Spanish wool, iron stays, hoops, high-heeled shoes and bolstered hips shall incur the penalty of the law in force against witchcraft and like misdemeanors, and that the marriage, upon conviction, shall stand null and void."

As late as 1945 a Tennessee state senator actually introduced a bill (in the Tennessee legislature) which would make the use of lipstick a felony. He gave no reason, but I suspect he went to a party and got WHUMPPED, and then went home and got whomped by his wife.

And the battle goes on. A mere nine years ago a London dentist posted this sign outside his office: "Lipstick. I will not attend to any woman with this filth on her lips. I am tired of getting it on my fingers and instruments. Before I attend to you, go home and scrub it off."

Small progress. Meanwhile, men, all we can do is stand there and take our WHUMPPS.

••••••••••••••••••••••

Such a to-do about the jet sonic booms over the city. I've heard them a few times and they don't bother me nearly as much as a number of other noises that are with us almost constantly. There are countless common sounds that are infinitely more annoying than the quick clap of a sonic boom. For example:

The thump-a-wump-a-wump in the washing machine that means wings on another $20 bill.

The sound of a car whose owner feels mufflers are for squares.

The uncontrollable rumble of your own stomach during the quietest moment in church.

The sound of your wife's voice when she finds those Christmas cards you forgot to mail.

The sound of the middle-aged juvenile behind you at sports functions who can't go anywhere without his blarehorn.

The wail of the ambulance siren on the night your teen-ager has the car.

The sound of unannounced company dropping in Saturday afternoon just as you've lain down for a nap.

The rumble of the commuter train pulling away just as you race into your gate.

The scrape of the razor Monday morning when you haven't shaved all weekend.

The dreadful moment when some dunderhead squats next to you, on train or bus, and turns on his transistor.

The neighbor's unleashed dog that picks your yard in which to bay at the moon; the voice of your child asking for help with trigonometry; the *awrrrawrrr* that makes it clear your car battery is dead; the terrible tinkle of the cash register in the supermarket after you've bought a week's groceries.

The honk of the silly goose behind you who uses his car horn as an all-around form of expression.

The slurp of the radio disk jockey who sips coffee while thumbing through a dated joke book.

The "whiter-than-white" shriek of doom in those detergent commercials; the dripping faucet at three o'clock in the morning.

The microphone that goes "eeeeeeeWUPP!!" just as you're launching into your speech.

Hailing a cab at the rush hour when the fellow next to you can whistle louder than you can.

The busy signal on the phone after the caller has left an "urgent" message to call him back.

The snarls of some of those fly-by-night folk-singing groups (and why don't they fly away?).

For those with claustrophobia, the sound of the plane door closing just before takeoff.

The alarm clock. Any alarm clock. Anytime. Anywhere.

And for those who write columns for a living, the ominous voice over the shoulder: "Twenty minutes to deadline."

••••••••••••••••••••••

I had an interesting phone conversation the other day with a pregnant lady. In a little while, she explained, she would be having her baby, and her husband wanted to be in the delivery room when it happened.

Her husband, she said, felt that the moment of fatherhood was a rare, sublime experience and it was something of a duty to be on hand when it happened. It was his feeling (the wife admitted that he had read this somewhere) that a husband should be a witness to the ordeal of his mate at a time like this. She quoted him as saying: "Men don't know what mothers go through, and they should."

The lady then explained that while she admired her husband's motives, and gave him good marks for courage, she felt a little disturbed about his attending the delivery. Did I, she wondered, have an opinion?

My opinion is that there are times when a husband should make himself scarce. And the moment of birth is one of them. Any full-grown male who doesn't know what mothers go through has to be a witless clod who's been hiding in the attic.

I do not demean the motives of the man who wants to be present. In a way his devotion is admirable. But in another, it's more than likely a clumsy nuisance. I'm not referring now to the desire for privacy which is natural for most women, though this is plainly an important factor (for most women, the fewer people around the better).

What I refer to is the matter of safety and comfort. While

birth is a common experience, it is still a matter of delicate medical attention—before, during and immediately afterward. It is my feeling that the mother, her doctor, and the attending nurses are functioning as a team that has enough to concentrate on without the hazard of unneeded distractions. And the husband fussing around is a decided distraction.

Certainly there's nothing for him to do. He won't be asked—thank heavens—to pitch in and help. He'll just stand there, possibly inviting a nervous trauma, in everybody's way. I don't believe that most doctors would appreciate his presence; their one concern is mother-and-baby.

In some cases where the father was allowed in the delivery room, it's a matter of record that it was an unpleasant experience all around. Some fathers have fainted or become ill—and that's all mother-to-be needs at a time like this: a conked-out husband.

The problem is becoming common enough for the State of California to have made it a matter of legal discussion. Formerly, fathers were barred from delivery rooms on the West Coast, but one potential papa made it a test case. The state ruled, just recently, that henceforth fathers may be admitted. So much for one legal aspect.

In the final analysis, I think that if the mother feels the least bit queasy about it, the old man should get lost. If it becomes a matter of disagreement between the couple (what a time to argue!), I think the attending doctor should make the decision.

In the case of the lady who telephoned me, it is clear that she is queasy about it. That being the case, her comfort and peace of mind—not the husband's curiosity—should be the prime concern. He should mark time in the waiting room, with the other nail-chewers, figuring how he's going to get him/her/them through college.

●●●●●●●●●●●●●●●●●●●●●

I like the commuter train I use in and out of Chicago morning and night. It runs on time, the seats are comfortable and the price is right. But best of all, I think, this Burlington R. R. train carries the most fascinating fraternity of commuters the suburbs have to offer. Does your line have these typical travelers?

Humphrey Huffandpuff: Invariably, this specimen makes it just before the doors slam shut. He collapses into the seat next to you, eyes bulging, tongue dropping, and his face a deathly purple. For the next twenty minutes he emits nothing but wheezes, gasps, and choking rattles. On reviving, he spends the rest of the ride tucking in his shirt, lacing his shoes and combing his hair. Occasionally he discovers that his socks don't match. He has another pair just like them at home.

Darryl Deadbeat: When the conductor strolls by, he develops an intense interest in the passing scenery or in his fingernails. He hopes the conductor will figure him as already punched. On days when he scores a free ride, he treats himself to an extra martini at lunch.

Nathaniel Nasaldrip: This one has a perpetual cold, but he boasts out loud that he's never missed a day's work through sickness. His fellow passengers, however, miss many days because they can't duck the germs he coughs at them.

Fauntleroy Fancyfoot: He enjoys guessing precisely where the doors will open at his home station, and when the train appears in the distance he begins to pivot and shuffle and soft-shoe all over the platform. He has an excellent record. He also has monumental blisters on both heels.

Lenny Lovelylungs: This specimen abhors smoking, yet for some reason he will avoid the thirteen non-smoking cars on the train and sit in the solitary smoker. He then proceeds to dilate his nostrils, frown and blow your smoke away with his newspaper. An odd one.

Reginald Royalflush: The moment this character sits down, out comes a deck of cards. He loses at least three dollars each trip and can't understand why his children have the rickets.

Quentin Quithabit: This is the guy who gives up smoking twice a week. But he borrows at least five cigarettes on each trip (saving two for the office). He has an interesting bank account.

Hugo Hungerpain: He comes aboard loaded down with Danish pastry, an orange, and a paper cup of take-out coffee. When the train jerks, coffee and crumbs will dribble onto your trousers. Breakfast done, he will calmly open his brief case and nibble on his lunch. He has a hard time getting life insurance.

Gladstone Gloomygus: His day was ruined the moment he struggled out of bed, so he doesn't see why yours shouldn't be. He regales you with stories about his domestic problems, unruly children, crabgrass, the high rate of heart ailments, his stupid boss, and a persistent pain in the pit of his back. Then he unfolds his paper and mutters that the world is in an unholy mess. Any moment, you fear, there'll be a derailment.

Maurice Musclebound: This bore forces you to hear every detail of his golf game, certain that you're thrilled if he scored a niblick on the ninth par, or whatever it is that golfers do. Especially obnoxious in the wintertime when he goes on about slaloms and things like that, dropping cigar ashes all over your coat.

Wilbur Wearybones: As soon as his fare is paid, his head falls on your shoulder and he's sound asleep. Just can't break the television-late-show habit.

Cynthia Seatsaver: At least one like her on every train. Dreadful.

Percy Pinchpenny: Avoid this one. Won't buy a newspaper. Borrows half of yours. In time, he'll get friendly. You'll weaken and invite him home to dinner. There he'll meet your daughter. Courtship starts. He'll ask you for her hand in marriage. And a guy who can't afford a paper—you want *that* for a son-in-law?

Bearing up with these companions is a much easier task than motoring to work on the tollways and expressways you can see from the train window. There, you'll run into—or be run into by—the likes of:

Terence Tanglefoot: The floorboard of his car is littered with such items as old sneakers, golf clubs, leftovers from drive-in snacks, and innumerable traffic tickets. His foot never knows if it will land on the brake pedal or accelerator: it just hovers around and hopes for the best. That's why he gets so many tickets.

Glendon Globetrotter: He wants to impress people. His windows are covered with decals from the Tennessee Smokies, the Kentucky Caverns, the Seattle and New York World Fairs, and other places. He buys them in novelty shops. Apart from going to Chicago, he has never been further than the suburb adjoining his own.

Howie Houndslave: This character can't go anywhere, not even to the corner for cigarettes, without his dog. It sits up front, nestles in his lap and licks his face while he's driving. Occasionally he leans over and pats the beast—at sixty miles an hour. He is proud of being an animal lover, a passion which keeps him from having much concern for the human beings on the road.

Luke Lookmeover: He has a $7000 foreign job, wears a beret, and sometimes reads a peekaboo magazine while driving. He considers himself the typical urban male and resents it when an ordinary American car comes close to him. His whole life revolves around his automobile. His wife drives a bicycle.

Dorian Doodad: This specimen never grew up. His windshield is alive with all sorts of clever things—toy skeletons, Hawaiian Kewpie dolls, baby shoes, king-sized dice, shrunken heads, and Batman puppets. Sometimes, on a clear day, he can almost see his own hood.

Wally Wallflower: This fellow's problem is that he's just not popular and suffers from intense loneliness. When he sees you in front of him, he drives up to within seven inches of your rear fender—and stays there. He doesn't understand why you don't appreciate his company. You often read about him on the obituary page.

Lennie Lanehopper: A natural candidate for the couch, he can't make up his mind which lane in the expressway he really likes. He tries them all, for half a minute at a time, in a continuous crisscross that sets off a chain reaction of collisions behind him. He doesn't believe in directional signals and, besides, what are *you* doing on *his* expressway?

Basil Bazoom: Lacking any talent, he draws attention to himself with noise. His car has no muffler, and his exhaust system has special equipment that belches sound which would put an astronaut to shame. His horn can drown out the whistle of the *Queen Mary,* and he can't drive unless the radio is on full blast. For him, ecstasy is a pair of screeching tires.

●●●●●●●●●●●●●●●●●●●●

I have before me three of those best-dressed-men's lists and, heavens to cummerbunds, Chicago's Mayor Richard Daley made all three.

No, I'm not jealous. But it does seem odd for one mayor to bag a trio of trophies like that in one year. It has plainly been a big year all around for the Democratic machine.

If you're a nut on civic pride, I suppose it's nice that Daley is the nation's best-dressed mayor. But are these polls truly representative? Did *you* vote? Have *all* the mayors been looked over? No.

Take Gavel P. Quorum, for example. For thirty-two years Quorum has been mayor of East Bylaw, Kentucky, and not once have the tailors checked his garb. "It's all politics," snapped Quorum, who runs on the Socialist-Prohibition ticket. "And it's publicity, too. My tailor never makes the gossip columns, and tailors make the gossip columns in Chicago."

Daley's Top-Ten-best-dressed colleagues include a prominent surgeon, and this doesn't sit well with Dr. Catnip McRabies, founder of and doctor-in-residence at Kennel and Kage Konvalescent Klinic. Says he:

"It's snob appeal, because veterinarians never make those lists. Anyway, this best-dressed doctor business is nonsense. Who ever heard of a badly dressed doctor?"

Also on the list with Daley was a best-dressed advertising executive whose selection nettles Gregory Grayflannel, account chief with Footloose, Nosecone and Balding. Grayflannel, currently stuffing midgets into washing machines, refuses to be seen anywhere without his Stay-in-Vietnam cuff links. "They're a liberal outfit," he snorted.

As best-dressed actor, the Custom Clothiers chose James Garner, whose current movie ads feature him in polka-dot shorts. But they never even considered the noted Shakespearean actor, Profile Upstage. It's true that Upstage is on his uppers at the moment, but he did make sartorial history some time back. Sorely in need of a morning pickup after a heroic binge while on a Chicago visit, he reeled into the Pump Room with his trousers back to front—setting off a trend to the rear-view zipper. Unfortunately, the style was adopted by women instead of men, and Upstage received no credit.

Nevertheless the history of the tailors' Top Ten is intriguing. Among frequent winners has been Harry Truman (chief executives always make the lists), who would reward the tailors by donning sports shirts so loud they could be heard in Hawaii (where they were promptly banned). Another winner was Adlai Stevenson, cited for "representing the Democratic party but dressing like a Republican" (after much soul-searching, Stevenson poked a hole in the sole of his shoe and destroyed the image).

Baseball's Lou Boudreau got the honor in both 1949 and 1951 and was so mortified he abandoned the game and fled to the announcer's loft in Wrigley Field. In 1949, the list of the New York Custom Tailors and Designers Club was headed by Harold Stassen and the Ritz Brothers (honest). Nobody knows what happened to the Ritz Brothers after that. Nor to Stassen, for that matter. Two years later, Leo Durocher placed tenth on a list and was heard to hiss: "What did I tell you. Nice guys finish last."

A few years ago the British fashion magazine, *Tailor and Cutter*, gave the top nod to Marshal Tito. The portly Yugoslav was so elated he flew to Moscow and bought twenty new suits—with American funds.

Nor was that the magazine's quaintest choice. In 1953 it listed England's Prince Charles, who was, at the time, all of five years old.

But my favorite is the Fashion Foundation's 1961 list which included nonconformist painter Raymond Duncan and John F. Kennedy.

Duncan, eighty-nine-year-old gaffer and brother of dancer Isadora Duncan, removed his pants in 1909 and donned a toga. And a toga he's worn ever since.

••••••••••••••••••••••

If you go to a party and there's a psychiatrist or two among the guests, my advice is—leave early. For you might straighten your tie and expose yourself as a repressed psychopath with a secret death wish. Or you might jiggle your ice cubes from left to right (instead of from right to left) and give away your abnormal guilt complex.

Now it's conceivable that your tie needs straightening. And it may be that you twirl the ice a certain way to avoid splashing your hostess. But this means nothing to some psychiatrists who see a motive (usually sinister) in every human activity—from the way you frown in thought to the way you vote.

You can't pick up a magazine these days but some psychiatrist is in there with an article about some new motive for ordinary behavior. It's a rare conversation show on television that doesn't have a psychiatrist on the panel who's expected to analyze any subject that comes up—including some about which he knows less than nothing.

(Perhaps you've heard the type: "Ah, yes, Napoleon was

very short in stature, hence self-conscious, hence overly ambitious"—followed twenty minutes later by: "Ah, yes, De Gaulle is very tall, hence self-conscious, hence overly ambitious.")

In less than an hour yesterday, reading two separate magazine articles, I discovered why people tip (or don't), and why people prefer one nut (no pun intended) to another.

You didn't know, did you, that the public sees something sinful about nuts? A psychiatrist, after a two-year study (honest, two years), reports that nuts suggest overindulgence, and if you prefer the more sophisticated nuts like cashews or almonds over the humble peanut, it means you have "violent, suppressed guilt feelings."

Says he: "Everybody thinks he's worthy of peanuts, but few consider themselves good enough for cashews."

It was also discovered that peanut-munchers are considered "square, dull and unimaginative" by people who don't touch the stuff. On the other hand, peanut-eaters judge those who prefer cashews as being introverts.

This is such a hot discovery that a large Massachusetts nut company is coming out with a new mix—55 per cent cashews and 45 per cent peanuts. Why? "To meet both social strata halfway," says a company spokesman.

(I don't especially care for nuts, being a licorice man myself. The simple reason is that I have pretty fair spaces between my teeth and nut-eating drives me nuts. But I suppose some psychiatrist will contend the real reason is that I had a disgusting childhood.)

Another psychiatrist—busy rascals, aren't they?—reports that the psychology of tipping is "part boast and part guilt" and—get this—it reflects the need to "buy absolution from the gods who, in this case, are the servants." By serving you, they hold you in their power and may purposely embarrass you so you'll try to win their approval.

That's why, the psychiatrist explains, a well-bred person is generally a small tipper and the social climber overtips—and the less secure you are, the more you'll tip.

Incidentally, the worst tippers are doctors, musicians, actors, politicians, and traveling salesmen in that order. The biggest tippers (and, if psychiatry is right, the most insecure characters) are bookmakers, gamblers, restaurant owners, and clothiers. Women are the more sensible tippers because they have less need to prove themselves that way.

Having come this far, I withdraw my advice about leaving early if there's a psychiatrist at the party. Instead, stroll around gnawing at peanuts and almonds, and give everybody a tip on the stock market.

••••••••••••••••••••

Despite the calendar and the snow on the ground, I'm heartened by the thought that spring can't be very far away. The perennial controversy over the wearing of beards by students on campus is with us again, and this is the harbinger of the days of nature's reawakening.

I am not a beard buff myself, but if one must be worn I've felt it doesn't seem unsightly on a well-proportioned, middle-aged man of some intellectual stature who has accomplished something. Few sights are more hilarious than a hopeful stubble hanging from the chin of a short, fat nineteen-year-old who doesn't know yet whether he'll grow up to be a public relations officer in the poverty war or a conscientious objector in the other one.

There are places where premature beards are better not looked at. One is on the extreme liberal who starts to fidget if a conversation goes ten minutes without the subject of

McCarthyism coming up. He's convinced that "society" is responsible each time some shiftless punk caves in an old lady's head in the subway for cigarette money, and he justifies his beard as a protest against society's ills. "I'm revolting," he explains. He sure is.

Nor do I like a beard on the congenital misanthrope who not only hates the world—especially this part of it—but can't stand the sight of his own face in the mirror. With a luxuriant growth covering the lower half, and a Beatle-type hairdo almost covering his eyes, his burden is lightened. The only trouble is he keeps bumping into things, making him hate the world all the more.

I know a sloppy eater whose beard always carries the remnants of his last meal, and he happens to be a devotee of Camembert cheese. His greatest hazard is strolling through the busy Loop streets where the pigeons dive-bomb him from all sides, seeking cracker and pickle tidbits. People stare as he ducks and weaves, hissing, "Shoo! Shoo!"

Sadly for some, growing anything beyond a fuzz is a physical impossibility so they become out-and-out cheats and wear a falsie—an artificial item actually introduced in England a few years ago. Their biggest nightmare is getting it caught in a revolving door.

One distressing aspect of the first-beard project is that most wearers don't realize that after washing one's beard one shouldn't venture out for a while because a beard takes an interminably long time to dry. I once sat across the table at a dinner party from a fellow who had obviously just washed his beard. The water kept dripping down to his jacket, and occasionally plopped into his soup, and he seemed flattered that people couldn't take their eyes off him.

One beard-wearer once confessed that he had grown a beard in order to save fifteen minutes shaving time each morning. He had hoped to put the time to practical use, like performing yogi exercises or writing poetry. Instead, he spends twenty minutes before the bathroom mirror, admiring and trimming the foliage.

At one time the beard on campus was the mark of non-conformity. Now it has become the mark of the sheep, and the non-conformist is the one who shears himself.

••••••••••••••••••••••

Spring, as every young man knows, is when his fancy lightly turns to what's been on his mind all winter. It is also other things:

Spring is when you come out of hibernation and speak to your neighbor for the first time since Christmas Eve.

Spring is when the yard is finally snowless and you come upon seven mittens (none matching), the snow shovel you borrowed in November, and fourteen Christmas cards that never did make it to the mailbox.

Spring is when you realize that the income tax deadline is no longer months or weeks away. It's like right now.

Spring is when you look at buds on the trees and get a warm feeling. Then you look at the storm windows and gag.

Spring is when you take the driver out of the golf bag, take a magnificent practice swing, and discover the spelling of sacroiliac.

Spring is when the Christmas bills come home to roost—most of them stamped: "PLEASE. Fourth Notice."

Spring is when the ladies trot off to the dress shop and come home crestfallen. It's diet time again.

Spring is when you promise that next winter you'll keep your New Year's resolutions to yourself.

Spring is when you wonder if you're not getting a little too old for tennis.

Spring is when you get your first look at the naked lawn and curse every dog in the neighborhood.

Spring is when your wife buys a new purse, then announces that next week she'll get the gloves, shoes, hat, and dress to go with it.

Spring is when you take the four bikes out of the garage and every one of them has a frozen flat tire.

Spring is when your neat, meticulous neighbor stares painfully at your emerging crabgrass, shakes his head, and walks away muttering.

Spring is when it hits you that you paid $49.95 for the barbecue pit and used it only once last summer.

Spring is when you go into the hardware store for a nickel's worth of nails and come out with a fortune in paint.

Spring is when the little ones insist that the sun is shining and why can't they go to the swimming pool?

Spring, if you're a student, is sitting in the park with a terribly guilty conscience.

Spring is an ugly, disgusting lawn mower staring at you in the garage.

Spring is when you worry about your teeth and hope that the dentist is on vacation.

Spring is when you remember when an Easter egg cost a nickel.

Spring is when you take a deep breath outside, feel ten years younger—then realize that a full year has gone by since last spring.

••••••••••••••••••••••

There was plenty of big news during that history-making power blackout in New York. There were lots of little happenings, too, but you didn't hear about them because the big ones got all the headlines. This, then, is to update you on little-known events that occurred on that Black Tuesday:

A fellow in a bar was doing justice to a double Gibson. The contact lens on his left eye fell into the glass just as the lights went out. Later that night he couldn't figure out why he was crying so much, until he discovered what he had retrieved and tucked into his eye was not the lens, but a peel off the cocktail onion.

One of those wild-eyed, bathless Vietniks burned his draft card at the corner of Fifth Avenue and Forty-ninth Street, and drew a record crowd estimated at 7,432,684. It was the only light in town.

Because the lights stayed on in New Jersey, just across the river from New York, pictures of the lighted scene were shown on coast-to-coast television. This is the first time that the breath-taking skyline of Newark, second only to that of Drycreek Junction, Arkansas, for architectural stimulation, has received the national exposure it deserves.

Jackie Gleason, relaxing in a restaurant, downed a glass of water by mistake, and the shock to his liver has kept him bedded ever since.

William F. Buckley, Jr., unsuccessful candidate for the mayoralty of New York City, stamped his foot and snapped: "I am *not* responsible, and I am *not* a sore loser!"

John V. Lindsay, who won the mayoralty, had the worst nightmare of his life. He dreamt that the blackout had occurred on election night, while the ballots were being counted–Chicago-style.

Forty seconds after a plane left the runway at LaGuardia Airport, the lights went out. At that moment a passenger looked out the window and said to his seat companion: "These new jets sure make time, don't they?"

On a subway train stalled in the Bronx, a pickpocket was observed picking his own pocket.

A newly married couple checked into the bridal suite just as darkness struck, whereupon the man turned to his wife and said: "Oh, fudge! Now I'll miss 'McHale's Navy.'"

A young guitarist with a Beatle hairdo rushed into a barber shop and shouted: "Quick! Take a little off the bangs."

The celebrated stage actor, Profile Upstage, signed an autograph in Times Square only to learn later he had signed a check made out to cash for $150.

The blackout interrupted an aging playboy while an electric toothbrush was massaging his teeth. He finished the job by hand and was promptly felled by exhaustion.

A foreign art-movie buff strolled into a theater featuring a Federico Fellini film, sat through two hours of black-on-black, and told an usher on the way out: "It's not much on action, but is this guy ever symbolic!"

A reporter on a New York City newspaper got a handsome raise when he typed out a story in the dark. He was the only newsman on the floor who didn't use the hunt-and-peck system.

Slaves of habit, New Yorkers kept staring at their black television screens. Next day, the Nielsen rating service reported that "Bonanza" had toppled into second place.

A pair of lightning bugs buzzed Manhattan en route to Maine and 8,000,000 pairs of hands frantically clawed the sky.

And all in all, New Yorkers found it simpler to light a candle *and* curse the darkness.

•••••••••••••••••••••

I wonder if it wouldn't be a good idea, at this point, to do away with Santa Claus.

I know the suggestion sounds shocking, and I speak as

one in whose house Santa Claus has been a fairly important personality at Christmastime.

But I feel he should be quietly removed from public gaze because it's a miserable fact that he has already been all but abolished as a symbol for children. This has been accomplished by adults who have wanted him for themselves, to use commercially.

Now I'm not advocating the total elimination of the Father Christmas image. I only urge that he be mercifully exiled from the public domain in which he's been thrown, stumbling and embarrassed, to become a grotesque caricature of something that was once gentle and warm.

I would like to see Santa Claus return to the days of our childhood, when he was what our imagination made him—a friendly man of warmth possessed of certain blessings that we could never quite categorize, who was never seen—except through the eyes of the heart.

He was all things to everyone, but something special to you and me—because he was simply what our dreams and hopes made him. What is he now?

I'm told there are a couple of "songs" entitled "Santa Claus Is a Dirty Old Man" and "Santa Claus Is a Fink."

What is he now? Ask the advertising industry, which has stolen him away from the imagination of millions of children the world over. His face begins to appear in store windows and printed page ads and billboards and on television as the summer leaves begin to twirl to the ground. We've ruined this thing in such a way that children now are doing their Christmas asking long before the traditional day of saying thanks.

What is he now? He is any of hundreds of guys who go to a special "Santa Claus School" in the fall to learn how to handle youngsters who pull his beard. The operations of this school were revealed on a 6:30 P.M. program the other night—a real thoughtful performance at the children's hour. And just a half hour later, Santa Claus was an actress on a video mediocrity called "Pete and Gladys." If there's anything more unpalatable than a woman dressed as Santa Claus, with a pillow beneath the red coat, I can't evoke it right now.

What is Santa Claus today? In most cities you can take your child on a half-hour walk and encounter a dozen Santa Clauses—some of them rheumy and unpleasant. I wonder what goes through the mind of the child when he's seen four of these old fakes in ill-fitting, sometimes unclean costumes in one hour.

In some communities I have seen whole platoons of these seasonal frauds dotting large intersections, bell-clanging for money. Of course it's for a good cause, but again I'm wondering about the child's thoughts.

I've also seen Santa Claus on Christmas cards, getting himself tickled and pinched by a bunch of bikini-clad harridans.

Father Christmas indeed. I don't blame Scrooge for summing it all up with one word: Humbug!

When I urge the abolition of this decrepit travesty, I refer to the Santa Claus we know today as we long for the one we remember from our yesterdays.

And now that we adults have made him a money-splendored thing, let's cease the ridicule and return him to the hearts of the children, where he belongs.

Come to think of it, old Scrooge may have had a point with all that humbugging at Christmastime. There are so many things that today are unpleasant about the season that's supposed to be jolly, I've wanted to say bah! many times. I've felt like that since the hard-sell commercialism took over in the early days of November.

What's pleasant about having to buy dozens of cards,

most of them much too expensive and many of which you'll be sending to the folks across the street or at the adjoining desks in the office?

And just when you think the revolting stamp-licking is over you receive another handful of cards at the last minute and you know yours won't reach them until after Christmas Day.

And then there's the marbles-in-the-belly feeling that you're spending too much money, and that you'll suffer for these commercial hysterics in January when the bills pour in. This is fun?

And I can't see much thrill in fighting the jostling crowds in the crowded aisles of department stores whose clerks seem to have dissolved behind the counters. It's pretty awful when you have to light a cigarette to get a clerk running to you.

And the tree. Eight dollars for a malformed cluster of droopy branches that gives you the fire-hazard willies during the night. And the bulbs that keep burning out just as the stores close for the weekend.

And that silly ritual of making the outside of the house look like a third-rate circus front. Who started that uncouth custom of sending out "judges" to look over your decorations? Who wants a prize, anyway? It only goes to the naïve who spent the most money on electrical gadgets. Why don't those fool judges go away?

And all the while, more so each year, that guilty, nagging feeling that there is less of Christ and His birthday and that willingly or not you're taking part in making it that way because everybody else seems to be doing it.

And the children. They've asked for this and wished for that but mostly they've wanted to know when it was coming and how do you explain the length of a week to a three-year-old?

And the blaring radios in the rooms and in the cars and in the stores until, after six weeks, Good King Wenceslas has become a thunderous bore.

And the Santa Claus image, stolen from the imagination of the children by the money-makers who have turned him into an ugly farce with dollar signs where the dancing eyes should be. So many displeasing things.

Yet, deep down, we have to quietly tell ourselves that there are worse things about Christmas.

Like being born in a stable, for instance . . .

The tragic lantern

During the year soon ending I have found myself snapping off the radio with a frequency that would, if I were in the business, frighten me.

I turn off the radio when I can hear the fellow at the other end slurp his coffee. Nor can I share his enthusiasm when he chomps into a doughnut (or is that just the way some of those fellows talk?).

I turn off the radio when, with an oral leer, the pinhead in the studio slips across a near-off-color joke or remark—especially when he's addressing himself to the youngsters dressing for school.

I turn it off when the station delivers three commercials in succession ("we'll spin that little old platter right after *this* message").

I turn it off during the "headline news" yammered out by screaming mimis (". . . and firemen estimated the damage at $400!! MEANWHILE IN VIETNAM IT WAS LEARNED . . .").

I turn it off when the dolt at the other end gushes that the visiting celebrity has been playing to a "packed house" in some local clip-joint—when the truth is the third-rate songstress or comic has been bombing out before large clusters of empty tables.

I turn it off when the syrup throat rumbling into my house or car tells me that the way to solve the Christmas shopping problem is to run out to a loan company and borrow $800—especially when the Santa Claus figure popping up in some shop windows a full week before Halloween has just reminded me that Thanksgiving can't be far away.

I turn it off when the same worthy insists the used-car dealer is robbing himself blind and pushing his family into the poorhouse with those bargains of his.

I turn it off when the "commentator" tells me that again in the interests of "public service" he'll again "explore" homosexuality or lesbianism or drug addiction next week, again with a "real homosexual" or a "real lesbian" or a "real addict" (are there any unreal ones?) on hand to give us the "true picture" of this "social problem"—for the fifth time in seven weeks.

I turn it off when the interviewee tells his host: "Yes, Marmaduke, it certainly is great to be back in my favorite city of Phila—, uh, Bost—, uh, Chicago."

I turn it off when the fifth-grader at the other end destroys any word that has three syllables or more.

I turn it off when the same segment from the same comedy album comes on for the fourth time in two days.

I turn off any station that persists in blaring (or singing) out its call letters every three and a half minutes.

I turn it off—promptly—whenever the cannibal music comes on (in this connection, some stations haven't been turned on in some homes since 1955).

I turn it off when the station delivers one of those pathetic movie-premiere things. ("Ah, here comes that popular tailor and man-about-town and first-nighter . . .") If these moochers want to free-load a suit of clothes, let them do it off the air.

There are so many times, sad to say, when turning off the radio is the only thing to do.

For me, one of those times (again) was last week when the announcer's pitch went like this: "Do your Christmas shopping EARLY! Look at the Three Wise Men! They shopped EARLY! Of course, there's no frankincense and myrrh around any more—but it's still a good idea to shop EARLY!"

Not where I live, friend.

••••••••••••••••••••••

Despite a vicious canard, none of my children has ever written this column. Except now. I am turning over this space to my sixteen-year-old son, Paul.

While evaluating one aspect of Chicago radio last week —the current fad for the nasally cacophonous yeh-yeh "music"—I was something less than charitable with one particular station which admittedly has a large lure for teenagers. I called it a pimple on the face of local radio.

Young Paul, who rushes loyally to my column each morning after the sports section, the comics, Ann Landers, the editorial page, the movie and play reviews, the news section, the crossword puzzle, and the obituary page, protested that there was another side to the story.

"You have the right to disagree with me," I said, "just as sure as Christmas—which you're looking forward to—is a week away."

He offered to write a rebuttal. "Even if it embarrasses me," I said, "it's your privilege—just as sure as I'll let you start driving the car next month, I think."

He hoped I wouldn't resent his equal time. "Just because

you're sweating out a raise in allowance," I said, "is no reason for you to worry about deflating me."

Thus assured of fair play, he wrote me the following memorandum:

"Dad: I think I can safely say that this station devotes most of the day to the teen-aged audience. Before and after school hours, the primary listeners constitute adolescents from junior high and high school. But who is it that complains about the station's music? Who is it that denounces disk jockeys, besides you, and condemns such 'trash'? The adult. This so-called mature generation takes on the privilege of criticizing a station that is for the most part not intended for adults.

"Who is really to decide what music is good and what is bad? What certain people think of a station does not apply to everyone, because each person is entitled to his own tastes. Those who don't particularly like the station don't have to listen to it. Adults seem to have the peculiar idea that all the teens do is listen to this station, which is far from true. I, as an example, listen on the average of one hour a day. My studies and other activities pretty well fill up the rest of my time.

"The Charleston and Big Apple swept the country some years ago and you older ones liked it. Rock-'n'-roll has the same effect on teen-agers. It is music that can be danced to. Consequently this station plays these types of records because of their popular appeal. I agree with you, though, Dad, in that there are certain disk jockeys that seem to go out of control when a microphone is placed in front of their mouths. I won't mention any names. But we're really being unfair in discriminating against a whole radio station for the actions of just a few.

"Finally, I would like to ask the adults to look at this controversy from the teen-agers' point of view, and to remind them that anybody who listens to music, even music with peculiar melodies, can't be all bad."

Well, that's his message. Unedited, unexpurgated and—sob—undestroyed.

Now many a father, after taking a rap like this from his scion, would promptly send the boy to bed without his supper. Not me. I intend to be fair about this situation. He'll sit at the table with me tonight as usual.

If eating crow is good enough for me, it's good enough for him.

••••••••••••••••••••••

I see where the members of the Federal Communications Commission have finally gotten off their ottoman and shown some action. They slapped television down for being "clearly derelict" in the matter of the crash-bang television series, "The Untouchables."

The rebuke dealt specifically with the program's handling of the saga of Al Capone, which clearly mixed segments of fiction with the unavoidable sordidness of fact.

This is an interesting development, and it brings up a challenging thought: Protests against "The Untouchables" have been in the area of extreme violence, and in the area of extensive concentration on individuals of Italian descent. The distress from Italians has been considerable but not, I think, without some justification.

Not much attention has been paid, publicly, to the fact that the protests of Italians against "The Untouchables" have been qualified by a just differentiation. I know a good many of these people—good people, all—and I have been in touch for three years with some of their national societies. I have found that their anger, almost invariably, was not directed at the representation of actual Italian-Americans.

It was directed at the tampering with actuality, the coloring-up of facts and the use of out-and-out fiction which have exaggerated the true stories. I am convinced that those who protested "The Untouchables" did so not because they were embarrassed by the truth, but because they were mortified by distortion. The FCC's action plainly justifies that complaint.

I was thinking of all these things the other day while reading a volume called *Four Centuries of Italian-American History* (you'd be surprised at what a columnist reads). It prompts me to suggest that the false image-makers on "The Untouchables" are overlooking the real untouchables.

I'd say that Leonardo Da Vinci was an untouchable, in many fields. So was Guglielmo Marconi—and astronomer Galileo Galilei, and Christopher Columbus, and philosopher Thomas Aquinas, and poet Dante Alighieri, and soldier Giuseppe Garibaldi, and composer Giuseppe Verdi, and physicist Enrico Fermi, and painter-sculptor Michelangelo Buonarroti, and statesman Camillo Cavour.

There are eleven refreshing episodes of real untouchables right there.

I was impressed, leafing through the book, with the countless contemporary Italian-Americans who have achieved the highest rung in scores of fields of endeavor. When the movies and television suggest that the typical Italian is an arrogant bootlegger whose mother pushes dope on the side, it's startling to learn how many have brought glory to themselves, and to this country, as governors and mayors, attorneys and judges, senators and investors, musicians and athletes, priests and poets, authors and builders, bankers and fashion designers, publishers and architects and so on.

Then there are the thousands in public service, working for the common good, whose names seldom make headlines. One of them is a neighbor of mine in the suburbs—Anthony Sorrentino, a supervising sociologist with the Illinois Youth Commission. He works with teen-agers with problems, and the resting days of Saturdays and Sundays mean nothing to him because the problems he deals with seldom take a rest. And there are thousands like him all over the country.

I'd say the Italians in this country have uncountable untouchables—and the movies and television should start counting.

••••••••••••••••••••••

It was as if, for three and a half days, the television set had been bordered in black.

For three and a half days since John Kennedy waved for the last time on a Dallas street, nothing but muffled voices choked, occasionally, by the cold clasp of personal grief. Here a catch in the throat of one high and mighty . . . There, the ill-repressed sob from a lowly one with no name.

For three and a half days, not once a word from the sponsor. And yet, one felt the unseen, rustling presence of the sheathed, tall-gaited figure. The sponsor was Death, and his message would long be remembered.

For three and a half days, not once the hearty sound of laughter. For the medium, like its audience, was in an agony of its own.

And now it is Tuesday—did all this happen but a weekend ago?—and the high-pitched voices and raucous laughter begin to return on radio and television. The harsh, commercialized cacophony is back.

Inexorably, the show must go on . . .

And as it resumes, two thoughts linger in the mind and brutally they blend into a paradox that seeks an answer:

One is that during the catastrophe that numbed the nation, television rose to its finest hour of public service.

The other poses the mournful question: Did it, perhaps, rise too high? In a zeal sometimes befuddled by panic, did it try to tell and show too much?

I am nagged by the horrible vision of the third, senseless killing—that of the young man said to be the assassin. His motives, the workings of his mind are now beyond recall. Could his death have been averted?

I believe that the chances for such a happening would have been considerably lessened if thoughtless people had refrained from making a spectacle of Lee Harvey Oswald. Was it necessary to inform the nation of each precise, split-second movement as he was being taken from one cage to another?

These were highly charged, emotional moments, moments to trigger the crippled logic of deranged minds.

Quite possibly the blame lies more heavily on the shoulders of the Dallas police force than on those of television. But there was, unmistakably, an arrangement between the two forces. Oswald's transfer was set up for television. It was a planned "production," publicized all too well. It was a sickening, disastrous error of judgment.

The same nagging thought assailed me that night. Some announcers repeatedly wondered on the air where John-John and little Caroline were sleeping as they spoke. One of them almost apologized because he couldn't disclose their whereabouts. Why? Was it necessary to know where these youngsters were? What about other sick minds, looking in, who might wish to "spare" them from the coming "ordeal?"

And why did announcers have to breathlessly inform everyone of the arrival time and place of world leaders? Was there not a gigantic risk in telling all? With all of the blood already spilled, was it necessary to place temptation before the glazed eyes of other madmen?

Why must we be such blabbermouths?

These matters aside, some moments on the screen will be inscribed forever on the minds of most of us: The young widow, her stockings still splattered with blood, trying to open the door of the ambulance carrying her husband's body . . . The President's two rocking-chairs being trundled out of the White House by a porter . . . Caroline, ever the little lady, standing stoically by her mother at the catafalque (and don't let anyone tell you that children don't understand) . . . The President's brother, hands in pockets, selecting a burial site in Arlington Cemetery . . . John-John bringing his hand to a salute as the cortege departed . . . And a weeping Cardinal Richard Cushing, bending to place a kiss on little Caroline's cheek.

I was with a five-year-old girl later, when an old film of the President was being shown. "He's not dead," she cried. "He's there!"

I guess he'll always be there.

●●●●●●●●●●●●●●●●●●●●●●●

A few days ago I started off a column with these words:

"One of these nights, Jack Paar could argue himself right off the air."

A few months ago, in a discussion of risqué material that sometimes threads through Paar's nightly program, the column said: "The explosion some night will blow Paar off the air."

I cite these predictions to illustrate how long ago—and how very recently—the storm warnings were sent up in this space. In some quarters, unfortunately, this is scorned as "slamming." In more mature headquarters, it is recognized as constructive criticism. It's a pleasure to report that Paar recognizes constructive criticism.

No matter. The prophecy has come to pass and there remains only its import. Paar told his "water closet" story, it was edited off the tape, and he's on his way to Hong Kong. Now this background:

In August of 1957, shortly after his late-night debut, I labeled Paar as a "blockbuster" (when most critics said he wouldn't last two months). Later, I nominated him as television's "Man of the Year" for 1958 (the man was making video news right and left). Since then I've often wondered why he never won so much as an Emmy Award nomination.

Having echoed this stand, I must now side with the National Broadcasting Company in its "censorship" stand on the "water closet" story. It's deplorable, however, that the whole thing will sink into an emotional morass further bogged down by the fact that it stems from a ludicrous incident. I suggest, therefore, that the public not lose sight of the most important factor in the entire mess:

What is at issue here is not the degree of bad taste within the joke which NBC blacked out. It is the principle of authority inherent to a network. It happens that Paar's story was not very harmful, and it appears that the button was indeed pressed in panic.

But I can understand that panic. To begin with—there has been a history of criticism associated with Paar's show (often balanced by viewers' claims that the criticism was unjustified). Further, television is now deeply involved in a long-awaited examination of conscience.

The medium has been blasted from all levels, ranging from government to individual. It has been accused, and rightly so, of abdicating its control over programs and turning itself into a money-mad landlord leasing the publicly owned time to anyone or anything able to afford it.

It's been a long-smoldering volcano which erupted with the shocking quiz scandal. Since then, television has entered the confessional and emerged to publicly promise to mend its ways.

Quite naturally, the Paar program was among the delicate areas where some disciplinary re-evaluation was brought into play. Now that it has happened, I do not intend to sabotage the network's intentions. I prefer to accept an error in critical judgment—if such there was—than snipe at the motives which I believe to be sincere.

I remain a Jack Paar admirer. But I devoutly hope he will not judge this issue on the tonnage and heat of angry letters flooding the network in New York. He must judge it as part of the broader, much more important principle that personal pride must cede to the public good.

A dramatic aid in understanding this troubled affair (and, while at it, in even sympathizing with Paar), is to pose this possibility: What if the joke HAD been an obscene one? This is worth the individual's reflection.

To say—as was suggested in the aftermath of Paar's departure for the Orient—that the public should be allowed to decide on an obscenity *after* it has been aired, is both dangerous and contradictory.

Many of us have demanded that the networks return to the helm. In recent weeks they have shown an inclination to do so. It's entirely possible that in the doing, they may hit a reef now and then and perhaps sail slightly off course. This is not of catastrophic magnitude. Not the voyage, but its destination.

I commend NBC for airing the aftermath of Paar's departure (which included some exceedingly painful criticism of its action), and for leaving the door wide open for Paar's return.

The pleasantly tempestuous Paar should—and likely will—put impulse into cold storage for a while, then warm up again to the good things that are both expected of and built into him.

••••••••••••••••••••••

The time has come to say something about Jack Paar's controversial pilgrimage to the Berlin Wall.

I put it that way because a lot was said (and made) of it before the fact—some of it unfair, some of it downright mean. Prejudging by prejudiced people far from the scene—and that includes some Congressmen and columnists—is usually dangerous. And the frequent aftermath—choking on crow—is always distressing.

I have questioned Paar's conduct on several occasions. I was opposed to his early embrace of Fidel Castro; I sided with the National Broadcasting Company when the network censored that notorious "water closet" anecdote, and I expressed displeasure over his nationally-aired feud with Ed Sullivan.

But even those who dislike Paar on general principles, or have had a falling-out with him, should not be blind to the traditional values of fair play.

I saw two of Paar's three telecasts from Berlin, and I thought both were excellent and in good taste. I'm told by people who saw the one I missed that it, too, was well done.

One point seems to have been ignored in the thousands of words I've read on the incident. Almost nightly for quite some time Paar has been saying on his program that he was going to Berlin. He spelled out exactly what he hoped to do while there. He made it clear that he would seek the aid of U.S. authorities. There was no subterfuge.

This is not to say that the Berlin journey was Paar's finest achievement. It was dangerous and pregnant with controversy, and Paar knew it. But several times before leaving he emphasized that he was not going there for the fun-and-games format that is typical of his program. As far as I am concerned, Paar kept his promise.

The result was that the programs were a restrained, low-key look at both sides of "the wall." The episodes showing actual escapes across the wall, and interviews with the escapees, were among the most dramatic I have seen on television.

In honesty, it must be said that there was some sloppy newspaper reporting on this matter. To suggest, by hearsay, that Paar would "not have been unhappy" if some flare-up had occurred is, to my mind, uncharitable and defamatory.

Because of Paar's temperament, I can understand the concern over this affair. But this does not excuse the low-blow criticism of an unseen event with a charge that Paar had commandeered U.S. fighting forces, with a flick of his finger, to help him stage a "production." If that were possible, it seems to me that the criticism should fall on the Defense Department.

Lastly, it seems strange that so much uproar attended the Paar voyage when the movie industry's use of our armed forces passes almost unnoticed. Only recently was passing attention paid to one Darryl Zanuck, currently producing a war movie in Europe. For this film (*The Longest Day*), Zanuck was able to enjoy the assistance of 1600 Marines and twenty-two ships of the Sixth Fleet operating in the Mediterranean.

Zanuck also had the use of 150 GIs who were diverted from West Berlin to France for him on orders of General Lauris Norstad, Supreme Allied Commander of SHAPE. For eleven days these soldiers "acted" with a cast that includes —steady, now—Paul Anka, Fabian, and Tommy Sands. Zanuck and Norstad are long-time friends.

Explaining this, the Defense Department says Zanuck's request was made in 1960, "at a time not of crisis." This is a weak excuse. For my part, there's been a crisis there since World War II. Certainly there was one in 1960.

Anyone for fair tennis?

•••••••••••••••••••••

Although television's high-money quiz-game programs like "The $64,000 Question" sank into tainted oblivion, there are constant movements afoot to bring back the gimmick that once held millions breathless for a few minutes each week.

Of course the ante will have to be upped because anything in the vicinity of $64,000 has become rather passé. I understand one proposed format is offering such first prizes as the states of Maine and Vermont (a package deal), an eighteen-month tenure as President of France, or the under-water rights to the Sahara Desert.

Be that as it may, such plans for tragic-lantern programing is the signal for frustrated losers, exhibitionists, and assorted oddballs to get into line. For this is a hazard of the quiz and giveaway show: it invariably attracts some strange ones. And sometimes the line between a genius and a psycho is a thin one indeed.

I once asked a producer of this type of entertainment why the program's screening systems were not sufficient to weed out the weirdies before their acceptance on the show. "You'd have to have psychiatrists to do the job," he said. "It takes a well-trained person to spot a phony."

I tend to agree. And another producer, Steve Carlin of the late "$64,000 Question" offers further proof. Among other things, Carlin's job called for turning back the fourteen-carat eccentrics.

Once, he tells me, he found himself impressed by a female applicant who seemed in fine fettle. Everything, including some weighty references, was going fine during the interview until she revealed that she and her bosom friends, President John Quincy Adams and Mrs. Adams, had just returned from a delightful vacation in Florida.

Another time, Carlin got worked up over an opera expert with a tremendous personality until the man said he would appear on the program only "if they don't bother me."

"They?" Carlin wondered.

"Yes," the man said, "the voices. I hear them all the time. I can hear them now—in your radiator. They give me a cold in the glands, you know."

On another occasion, Carlin had hold of what he called a "natural"—an elderly man with a beautiful head of white hair and a flowing beard the color of new snow. "He was heavenly," Carlin recalled, "and all the angles were there. He was the spitting image of Santa Claus. And you know what? His category was children's stories! What a combination!"

Until, during the routine test, Carlin asked him to identify the author of *Pinocchio*.

"*Pinocchio?*" the old gent wheezed testily. "What's that?"

Citizens who have misplaced their marbles are not the only ones, of course, who create problems. Carlin told me of the sweat he worked up with Salvador Dali.

Dali, a modernistic painter with unpredictable traits,

wanted to appear on "The $64,000 Question." Carlin was ecstatic, for imagine the rating a man like Dali could pull in the art category. Trouble was, Dali wouldn't go for that classification.

"My category," he rumbled, "is the horn of the rhinoceros."

Carlin coughed politely and invited Dali to elaborate. "My dear fellow," said Dali, impatiently, "the horn of the rhinoceros is the basis of all religion and philosophy. And even medicine."

Off to the library went Carlin to discover that the only horn that made any sense, if you cared to pursue this thing, was the horn of the unicorn—which at least had some mythological connotations that I'd rather not go into right now.

Carlin went so far as to consult with Northwestern University's Dr. Bergen Evans in Chicago, who knows more about the rhinoceros and such things than is proper for one man. It turned out that the rhinoceros doesn't even have a horn to begin with. An unaccountable piece of muscle is what it is.

Carlin tried to get Dali to submit to questions about things he knew best. "I," snorted Dali, "am the world's greatest living authority on the rhinoceros horn. My library is full of books on the subject."

Well, Carlin wondered, maybe he could look at some of those books?

"I should say not," Dali exploded. "That wouldn't be fair."

The argument went back and forth for some time and Carlin, to his credit, held his ground. In the end, he told Dali thanks anyway, but he couldn't use him.

"All right," said Dali, angrily flicking his mustache, "but you'll be sorry."

Later, Carlin's program was to make ugly headlines. Maybe Dali knew something?

●●●●●●●●●●●●●●●●●●●●

A Chicago television station this weekend starts taking another stroll down Misery Lane.

I mean here we go again with dope addicts, homosexuals, alcoholics, lesbians, abortionists, and girls who get "in trouble." The station's new series will look at these problems this month and next, with the afflicted individuals relating their unhappy sagas on camera. One program will feature a couple of out-of-town homosexuals and a "representative" from a Chicago "organization" of lesbians.

Before going further, let's make this clear: No one denies that these problems exist, and no right-thinking person wants them swept under the rug. Nor is there even the hint of a suggestion here that such programs are vulgar. They are directed to grownups and slotted for a late hour, and any mature person who can be corrupted by an adult conversation may as well leave the boat and paddle elsewhere.

But while we shouldn't turn our heads or hearts away from the individual's intimate problems, I wonder if we're not getting a little surfeited with them as a showcase. And I'm not singling out television.

Newspapers, magazines, books, movies and the stage have for quite some time, I think, become rather top-heavy with this sort of thing. It's good that it be explored. But one is tempted to wonder where exploration ends and exploitation begins.

No one can say that the various media have pussyfooted around these themes in recent years. Any adult who doesn't know, today, how or why a teen-age girl gets "in trouble," and how or why drug addicts and alcoholics get hooked has to have lived a pretty secluded life indeed.

Is it an urgent necessity that these unfortunates keep parading before the public eye, telling and retelling the same sad stories? Is the repeated use of bare-all exhibits actually solving anything, or is it a subtle form of transom-peeking?

We keep seeing unwedded girls, big with child, and certainly we share their anguish. But there are millions upon millions of teen-age girls who don't get pregnant, who study hard and help at home and volunteer at church and grow up to become fine citizens and good wives and mothers, and they seldom (if ever) get the spotlight (or want it).

We feel for the addict and wish him a new start in life. But wouldn't it be nice if, some time, television took a look at the ordinary citizen who gives a lot of his time and efforts and money and concern for the addicts?

I suppose the camera zeroing in on a lesbian has dramatic potential. But how about the shoe-store clerk who's going to spend next Saturday and perhaps part of Sunday pooping himself out for his community, or for some institution that doesn't even know his name? That unsung hero bit is fine, but how about a little song for him—just once in a while?

Some will retort with that tiresome whine that "society is to blame." For reasons that escape me some people seem to enjoy rubbing society's nose in the dirt for everything from the burning of U.S. consulates abroad to the shiftless punks whose credo is that purses are for snatching. I'm weary of that bleeding-heart bleat.

Society is you and I. And there are a lot of you's and I's who are good citizens, who support causes and problems with taxes and contributions, with time and effort, and many of these you's and I's are finding that they don't have much time, money, and effort left to care for their own.

These good citizens aren't about to drop what they're doing in these areas. But they'd be ever so grateful if the society-is-to-blame bleeders would zip their lips and shut up.

And I don't think they'd resent it at all if television would occasionally relate what much of "society" does for the unfortunates who get "in trouble."

•••••••••••••••••••••

It has prosaic clichés like death in the afternoon, and the brave bulls, and man's encounter with his soul, and all that jazz. And some folks, notably novelists and barefoot actresses, go to absolute pieces over it. But with all the ceremonial trappings—and it has more than initiation night at Soggy Corners' Loyal Order of the Wombats—a bullfight is simply a bullfight.

For two television hours the other night I watched six of them in succession, since they constitute the most touted series on the station that carries them—courtesy of videotape from Mexico. Square that I am, my reaction is that when you've seen one bull die you've seen them all.

The program format includes a panel of local bullfight "experts" who comment on the action in the ring while the tapes unreel.

Incidentally, it's not considered "in" to describe the panelists as fans, or even devotees. They are *aficionados*. Likewise, the cape is not a cape, but a *muleta,* and only an ignoramus would refer to the *estoque* as the sword.

Anyway, during this *corrida* (performance) the first *toro* (bull) pranced out of the *torile* (bullpen) into the *plaza* (ring), churning up the sand and oblivious to the color of the spectacle. All cattle are color blind, as everybody doesn't know, and the reason that the cape—uh, muleta is always red is to minimize the sight of blood.

Then a *novillero* (apprentice) astride a blindfolded horse lanced the bull's neck muscles with a long pike so the bull would not favor one horn more than the other against the *matador* (bullfighter). The horse is heavily padded. Formerly, when it was not, the bull would often disembowel it —a sight which tended to cut down on the sale of tortillas in the stands.

Next, the *banderilleros* (aides) ran up to the bull and implanted their *banderillas* (darts) into its shoulders, a procedure which enraged and weakened the animal. One of the aides looked like Buddy Hackett, and the sight of this fatso running tippity-toes toward the bull was something to see.

"This bull is too weak," complained one of the panelists. "He attacks the horse but does not push it."

"The matador isn't much," said another. "He's too nervous."

Well sir, you get a weak bull and a nervous matador and you start wondering what's playing on the other channels.

Eventually the bull stumbled and lay there, the sword stuck through the neck and into the heart. Then he rose, staggered halfway around the ring as if to show he was no patsy, and suddenly fell dead. The tape didn't show the aide sever his spinal cord at the base of the skull, just before the mules carted the carcass away.

The second bull, the panel decided, was also a bum because he pawed the sand "like a maniac" and had "the face of a cow." At one point he leaped the fence and rumbled down the runway. But there was no running away. He was herded back into the ring, and he crumpled in the sun.

The third bull received three swords in the neck, but none sank deep enough to pierce the heart. The fourth one did—and nobody on the panel said anything about the butterfingers with the cape—uh, muleta. The next bull put up such a fight that the matador was rewarded with an ear, and some aficionados threw their hats into the ring—just like a good many lunatics do in Chicago during the hockey games.

As the fifth bull waited for death, a panelist explained the true art of killing: The matador waits for the moment of truth when its head is down, opening a path to the heart through the separated vertebrae. The last bull, almost as bored as the television audience, vaulted the fence three times. "Such a coward!" exclaimed a panelist.

I only hope that later someone had a kind word for the beast, as part of it lay on the plate—between the potatoes and the peas.

••••••••••••••••••••

I've postponed saying anything about those two noisy things on television, "Shindig" and "Hullabaloo," in the melancholy hope that perhaps they might go away. Sadly, as of yesterday, they have not.

I watched each monstrosity once and could believe what I was hearing because the wretched caterwauling that passes for "popular" music is all around us these days. Radio has done a complete job of blaring its barbarism into the nation's homes.

But I could hardly believe what I was seeing, so I watched each program—if that's the word—a second time. I now feel prepared to ask my employers for a raise, for any normal person beyond the age of twenty who watches these mediocrities more than once deserves some sort of reward.

If there is anything more abominable than this exercise in teen-age vulgarity, I can't think of it.

In both programs watched, some male performers gave thinly veiled indications of homosexual exhibitionism.

How else explain the behavior of young men who wear

pants that seem the next thing to female leotards (and probably were sprayed on), fur vests, ruffled silk collars, and Prince Valiant haircuts, and who grimace and gyrate and toss their derrières like some fourth-rate bump-and-grinder and then smile soulfully into each other's eyes as they twist before one another?

One could almost forgive these people if some talent were in evidence. But the programs have the greatest collection of untalented performers ever assembled. Before a normal audience—devoid of hysterical girls paid (in tickets) for screaming—they would be hissed off the stage in four minutes.

Besides being nauseating, it's sad to see what the network executives are doing with the little girls they use as backdrops. These unfortunate creatures (about whose parents one has to wonder), attired in immodest dress for their age, are paid to fling their torsos and bosoms about like the semi-drugged harridans that stumble about the stages of fifth-rate striptease dens.

They're twitchers, the whole lot of them. Put them before a camera and the mouth twitches, and the neck, and shoulders, and the chest and waist, and the pelvis. Good grief, aren't there any healthy ones around?

Where the singing is concerned, the idea seems to be that the voices must be as unintelligible as possible. One group described by the host as "very famous Americans" went through one song where the only understandable word was "baby." On one show, Brenda Lee went to the other extreme—breaking the words in two ("than-hanks a lo-hot, I go-hot a bro-hoken ha-heart").

The dictionary describes *hullabaloo* as "a confused noise; uproar; tumult." That it is. It describes *shindig* as "a festive occasion with dancing." That it most decidedly isn't.

As one who happens to like normal teen-agers, I describe both these programs as musical and instrumental stench bordering on the lewd.

••••••••••••••••••••••

What follows will not be pleasant to write. It deals with a most delicate matter, but I think it needs to be said.

Perhaps the people whom it primarily concerns feel the same way, for I have received a three-page statement on the subject. It comes from Jacob Grumet, associate chairman of the civil rights committee of the Anti-Defamation League of B'nai B'rith. It's directed to my attention as a columnist.

Grumet deplores the fact that a "distressing number" of comedians are now combining offensive stereotypes of minority groups with sick humor to project "a morbid, outrageous and damaging picture of whole groups of Americans.

"The idea seems to be that anything goes for a laugh, up to and including jokes that suggest indecent or grotesque conduct on the part of clergymen." Grumet says this sort of thing is prevalent on television, in night clubs, and on records, adding:

"Recently more than 35,000,000 persons heard comedians on three television networks denigrating the rabbinate."

Grumet's concern is understandable. I have seen and heard a number of these loudmouths; they are a pollution, infected with moral and intellectual rabies. In night clubs their routines have almost no limit. Portions of their recordings are nothing but filthy wax. And they're trying very hard to slip their slime into television.

Shortly before he left his nightly program, Jack Paar had

on a comic who had been billing himself extensively as a former student of the rabbinate who switched to show business. He sneaked in a crude reference to sexual aberration and, when it brought no laughs, had the nerve to leer at the audience and say: "You're not with me, are you?" Paar turned away in pain.

The sad fact is that the majority of night-club comedians are of Jewish heritage and the guilty ones are in this group. Blending sex perversion and the clergy for the sake of a joke has not been a trademark of a Bob Hope or Jackie Gleason or Danny Thomas. Grumet's statement appears to touch on this with these words:

"Many comedians who combine gross, unfair stereotypes with sick humor are often themselves members of minority groups. Somehow, they think that this fact gives them special license to ridicule—in the most vicious ways possible—their own faith or religious institutions."

The situation has become so evil that case-hardened show business magazines are frantically calling for a stop.

I would like to see the leaders of racial minorities attack the problem by going right to the source—by directing their complaints to the individuals themselves, perhaps shaming them for lack of pride in their heritage.

And I would like to see less pussyfooting on the subject by show business columnists and show people generally. My mail shows complaints about radio disk jockeys who play portions of this garbage on morning programs. Some columnists too often piously refer to this sickness in such flabby terms as: "Comedian So-and-So is really great, really brilliant. It would be so much nicer if he weren't 'blue.'" This is cowardly poppycock. The guilty ones should be called what they are—dirty little minds—and invited to get out of town. And that should be the end of it. Their names shouldn't be mentioned so often in the columns. Why keep the sunshine of publicity on this squalor?

Sad to say, some of these repulsive characters not only are mentioned much too often in the columns, they manage to get on local television programs and radio interviews and discussion formats. The idea seems to be that they may be a little misguided, but they have a "social message" for the world.

This is a lackadaisical, cowardly, and meaningless attitude. Let's show a little courage. Most people are sick to death with this "mature" junk. They don't want it on the air.

Why don't men of decency who have influence stand up and be real men, and cut out this foul social cancer once and for all?

It isn't **ALWAYS** *funny*

The big plane rumbled through the blackness above my house about twenty miles from Chicago, and a few seconds later it plunged its seventy-eight people into the cornfield and eternity.

The searing flash was so strong, it was as if every light in the house had been suddenly turned on. From the window I saw the orange ball of flame hurtle upward, followed by what looked like a series of rockets bursting in flashes of falling fire over the calamity less than a mile away. The sky itself shuddered.

And within half an hour I saw a sight that brought shudders to the soul.

The morbid, lured by the smell of death, started their eerie cortege to the scene of burning flesh. The long, plaintive wail of the sirens told them this was a sight not to be missed, and they routed themselves from their beds (it was almost 1 A.M.) and trudged toward the gigantic glow.

They came by car, and on bicycles, and on foot. They came singly and in pairs and in family groups. And some of them carried their babies in their arms.

I stood there near the highway that separates my suburb from its neighbor, and watched them walk to the disaster in the glow of the lights from the fire trucks. I could hear their loud laughter above the din of clanging bells, and some of them looked as if they were hurrying to a picnic. Some ambulances almost had to stop, until the crowds moved off the road to let them pass.

One police officer who was on the scene within minutes told me later that he came upon a woman in a housecoat who was going through a wallet she had snatched off a body flung from the wreckage. As he pitched her off the area, this atrocious harridan whined: "Everybody else is doing it. Why can't I?"

Before reinforcements arrived to get some semblance of order amid the chaos, some of the flint-hearted visitors were trying to pass themselves off as deputies and photographers.

They sloshed through the mud and walked over the bodies and picked up pieces of metal and clothing as "souvenirs." What do they do with these things? Do they hang them up in the living room for the admiration of their friends?

Why do people flock to a disaster, knowing full well that they impede rescue workers and endanger those who might possibly survive? So they can regale their friends with eyewitness accounts? I asked a suburban police chief who was there:

"I've been a police officer thirty-eight years," he said, "and during a disaster there are always some people who stop acting like human beings. I can't explain it."

Eventually a guard system was set up, and cars were stopped at the big intersections near the catastrophe. Now it was past 2 A.M., and the cars were lined up bumper to bumper near my house and even on my street. The occupants left their cars on the driveways of strangers and joined the walkers.

I finally went to bed at 4:30 A.M. They were still coming as close to the area as they could at that hour. And the next day a man was on the scene with a little truck—selling ice cream cones and popsicles.

Death from the skies is a horrifying thing. If the bomb is ever dropped over here, there will be some fearful moments. But the fallout is not the only thing I fear.

What I fear is the band of fools in the processional of death who will come to look and laugh.

••••••••••••••••••••••

At long last, after many years, I was able to keep the promise I had made to myself. I was calling on the little girl whom nobody wanted.

She lies under the ground in Northwood Cemetery, just a few miles out of Hartford, Conn. I'm not sure just why I wanted to go spend a little time with her. I only know that when I heard of her I told myself that if I should ever be in Hartford I would stop by.

So I was in New York, and Hartford was just a short train ride away. And now I found myself on the gentle, green slope made warm by the afternoon sun. I stood and thought of "Little Miss 1565"—six years of age, blond, beautiful, and abandoned. She doesn't even have a name.

On July 6, 1944, she was among the more than six thousand people packed under the big-top tent of the Barnum and Bailey Circus playing a one-day stand in Hartford. At 2 P.M., bandmaster Merle Evans raised his arms for the opening number and the show was on. At 2:35 P.M., a strong southwest wind started rustling the flaps of the 75,000 square-foot tent.

At 2:40 P.M., Evans' eye was caught by a small flame dancing near the top of the tent, the size and color of an orange. He immediately stopped the music and called for

"Stars and Stripes Forever"—the sign, for the circus-wise, that danger lurked. But it was too late. In less than a minute the gigantic tent was an envelope of flame fanned by the wind, and within moments the big top was a holocaust of fire and panic.

One hundred and sixty-eight persons perished on that muggy, sun-seared afternoon, and more than 450 were injured. For long hours that night and the next day, hundreds walked by the uncovered bodies in the morgue to claim their own.

One body, that of a six-year-old girl with a beautiful face, bore a tag with the simple legend: "No. 1565." Most of the dead had been burned beyond recognition, but except for a bruise on the left cheek "Little Miss 1565"—as she was to become known—was not even disfigured. She had died of suffocation, probably where falling poles and ropes had blocked an aisle near the leopard chute.

And relatives and friends of the victims filed by the little cot, and looked at her placid, sleeping face. Not one stopped to say: "She's mine."

By the weekend the others had been buried, but "Little Miss 1565" lay on her cot, unclaimed.

Finally she, too, had to be laid away. But before she was placed into the ground—with no mourners except a few policemen—she was photographed, and records were made of her dental chart, her fingerprints, and her footprints.

In the months that followed these were sent out throughout the state and later to other states and across the nation. Surely someone would recognize her and come forward. No one ever did.

In all these years since the worst catastrophe in the history of the circus no mother, no father, no uncle or aunt or sister or brother has come up to claim "Little Miss 1565."

Yet she is not forgotten. The city of Hartford has cared

for her grave, and a neatly trimmed hedge in the form of a cross serves as background to her stone which bears the words . . . "her identity known but to God."

Three flower plants and a wreath lay near her stone the day I stood at her grave.

I wondered, as I stood there, how a pretty little child could perish and then become merely a number. Why did no one claim her? Why, even if she were unloved, did no one identify her if only for the crass reason of a lucrative lawsuit?

How could a little girl go so completely unnoticed?

Somewhere, someone has the terrifying answer.

••••••••••••••••••••••

A few days ago I received a letter from a woman reader who wrote: "We've suspected that you were pompous because of your notions on patriotism and flag-waving."

I don't intend to apologize for flag-waving because of malcontents who scoff at patriotism as an antiquated clump of corn. God help this nation if we ever become too self-conscious to touch hand to heart when the flag goes by.

But the lady who wrote in goes on to assume that because I like this country I must be a despicable Republican. When I came to this country, Harry Truman was the President, and I loved it here as much then as I do now. What sort of thinking is this that suggests that patriotism is a part-time, party-in-power thing?

Under normal conditions I would drop the lady's letter into the wastebasket. But on this historic election day, I have a few thoughts I'd like to share with her:

I am an American by choice—not by birth—who spoke the oath of citizenship a few years ago. You see things differently when you get yourself adopted, and you have perhaps a deeper appreciation of what others take for granted.

So I had become depressed—the word is nauseated—by the wail of sophisticates that this country has been going to hell in a golf cart. I guess I'm old-fashioned, but I can't share the sheeplike applause for saloon comics who've made patriotism a derisive word. I'm more concerned with what God thinks of this country than what the stone-throwing delinquents abroad, and our campus "progressives" here, think of it. Perhaps it's corny, but lately I had been longing for some lusty flag-waving.

It was refreshing, three months ago, to find it at the International Amphitheatre, hard by the Chicago Stockyards, where I attended my first national political convention. I loved every crazy, somber, screaming, gentle, chaotic, inspiring American minute of it. I watched it from every conceivable position—on the floor and high up in the broadcasters' booths and on a dozen television monitors simultaneously and even through the very eye of the video camera. And when the thousands bowed their heads in prayer or stood on their toes and cheered or raised their voices to "God Bless America"—I got lump after lump in my throat.

There were many memorable moments. For me, one occurred the night I slipped quietly into John Daly's ABC-TV booth near the rafters. Daly hadn't heard me come in as the session got under way. Gently he set down his earphones, turned away from the electronic gadgets, and said to his aides in the booth:

"Gentlemen, on our feet."

And Daly and his aides stood during the National Anthem and sang the words loudly, and remained standing during the presentation of the colors, and remained standing during the invocation. And after that long moment of reverence for their God and their country, they plunged into the maelstrom again. It touched me.

And it touched me when the American consul gave me my permanent visa a decade ago and said: "I hope you like living with us." I've had a love affair with this country since that day, and it gets more passionate with the passing years. I came here not knowing a single soul except a man I had corresponded with, but in two weeks I knew enough people to know I was home.

I was afraid. But the only time I stumbled was when I stumbled on opportunity, for it was all around me. All you had to do was take a crack at it. That was all the country asked.

I have seen genuine goodness in the hearts of the American people. I've seen the way they treat a stranger. I've seen the nation drop everything when the world was in trouble. And I've seen its people drop everything when a neighbor was in trouble.

But all this—and the majesty of the Smokies and the lovely face of Washington and the serenity of a southern street and the glory of the astronauts and the Grand Canyon from the air and the comfortable cars and the good schools and the health of the children and the beautiful women and the freedoms so rare elsewhere—this is only part of the story.

There is the deep faith in the greatness of this land and its future for those who care to look around for it—despite the hate-mongers among those who demonstrate in the streets. There is the knowledge that the faults and the wrongs won't always be there, for other faults and other wrongs have been removed with man's goodwill and with patience and with time.

It may be that the outsider—which I am, in a way—sees

and feels these things more keenly than the native. It may even be that he has more faith. I don't know.

I do know that I am about to vote in a presidential election for the first time in my life. This excites me. And the reason for the excitement is that voting is a very precious privilege. In some countries, millions of people haven't had that privilege for three generations or more. How much they would give to exchange places today with the grumpy sit-at-homes who won't vote because their man wasn't nominated.

What, after all, is patriotism?

It isn't the sight of the Statue of Liberty. It isn't a whoop-de-doo on the Fourth of July. Those are but symbols.

It's pride in each other. It's children safe in their beds at night. It's being able to scram your job tomorrow if you feel like it. It's having the right to laugh and play and speak and write and think and pray as you wish. It's liking it here. It's wanting to say thanks. It's contentment.

It's going into the private booth today and making your choice and cheering if he gets in, and closing ranks if he doesn't behind the one who does.

If this is flag-waving—long may it wave.

••••••••••••••••••••••

It was only a matter of time—like the length of a burial service—before television decided to exhume the Caryl Chessman story. A couple of producers are already scurrying around for money to bring this sordid affair into the American home.

There's activity in the movie bullpen too. A prominent actor plans a movie on the Chessman saga. For reasons known only to bleeding hearts, his movie will cover only

Chessman's twelve years in death row. In other words, what should be a crime-and-punishment study will center on the punishment and ignore the crime.

Lest television adopt the same distorted tack, I offer these thoughts:

In weeping over Chessman's execution (for kidnaping and sexual abuse of two women), let the camera go back to 1937 when Chessman was sixteen and convicted of three auto thefts, two burglaries, and two escapes from detention.

Let it pause on 1938, when Chessman was seventeen and convicted of auto theft and attempted burglary. Let it cover 1941 when Chessman's record lists thirty robberies, eight auto thefts, and two assaults with intent to kill. Let it focus on 1948 when Chessman was convicted of seventeen crimes —including robbery, burglary, auto theft, perverted sexual attacks, attempted rape, and kidnaping (I've been researching a lot of library records on this matter and I very much feel like getting soap on my hands).

Having done that truthfully, the movie or television script will then have asked an interesting question: If the death penalty is not a deterrent to crime, is imprisonment a better deterrent?

It's more than probable that the play will seek to highlight the "inhuman suffering" of Chessman's last-ditch appeals. In so doing, let it point out that Chessman was convicted twelve years ago, yet his lawyers were offering "new" evidence while the cyanide pellets were being dropped.

And I think an honest windup for the play would be a brief interview with one of Chessman's victims, a polio-stricken woman. Then the camera should visit the insane asylum where Chessman's other victim now lives. There's no death row there. I call it the living death row.

Finally, just before the last commercial comes on, I think

it would be proper if the teleplay climaxed with a superimposition of a Chessman quote—taken from one of the three books he was able to write during his "inhuman suffering." It goes like this:

"I became a criminal and an outlaw by choice."

If the play does these things, and shows an interest for accurate research and reporting—then I will attend it. Otherwise—no.

••••••••••••••••••••••

The main argument against capital punishment is that the fear of the supreme penalty is not a deterrent—that is, it does not diminish the number of murders.

Often this theory is advanced by some students of sociology (amateur and professional) who have never been near a potential killer. They don't know what it's like to have a bullet graze their skin, or the nose of a gun pushed into their ribs. They don't know what it's like to wait for death at the hands of a human beast.

Policemen who know these things have a different opinion as to whether the fear of capital punishment is a deterrent. One such is Sergeant Paul Jankowski, thirty-four, of the Chicago Police Department. This is his story, from the official police reports and from his own words:

On the morning of December 4, 1959, Jankowski and his partner were cruising on the Northwest Side of Chicago when they noticed a car with three occupants without a city sticker. They curbed the car and ordered the three men to step out for questioning.

The trio emerged, and two of them (all three were ex-convicts) whipped out revolvers and disarmed the two officers. Said one: "I'll kill you, you —— ——. You won't be the first —— —— that I rolled." Jankowski and his partner were ordered into the thugs' car, and the one who had not drawn a gun—who was later to save their lives—got behind the wheel.

As the car sped away, the first man said: "When we get to some out-of-the-way spot, we'll kill the ——." The officers pleaded for their lives. Jankowski told me he was "copping a plea for five kids I didn't have" (he now has two). But two of the three ex-cons were bent on murder. "We ought to kill the —— —— now," said the second man. "They're always putting people in jail for little —— —— things."

The third man broke the silence and told his partners that "cop killing" meant the chair for sure. But the gang leader said: "Let's get rid of these guys before we get caught with them." The second man said: "If we leave these —— out, they'll put more heat on our tail. Let's take them out to the country and kill them."

The car sped on, and again the driver told his pals about the electric chair. The conversation went back and forth about killing the officers and the danger of the chair. Says Jankowski: "I thought this was it. I was certain we were going to get it any moment."

But the driver kept nagging the two others that in Illinois killers got the chair. Eventually the car reached a lonely alley, and by then the gang leader had reached an agreement with the driver not to add murder to their records.

Jankowski and his partner were handcuffed to a fence from which they were later released by other officers who were now fanning out in the neighborhood, looking for the missing officers. The three thugs were captured minutes later after a gun battle (in which one policeman was shot). They are now in the penitentiary.

Jankowski doesn't feel he would be alive today if it were not for capital punishment.

Not all of these ordeals have fortunate endings for police officers. One ending remains indelible in the mind of another Chicago police officer, Lieutenant John Griffin.

It happened some years ago in Michigan, where two convicts had escaped from the state penitentiary. A state trooper came upon them on a highway. He, too, was suddenly disarmed and handcuffed to a post along the road.

While he stood there, helpless, the two fugitives (it was later learned) debated on whether to kill the officer. Finally, one said: "Well, in Michigan they don't fry (execute) you. The worst that can happen is jail."

And then they killed him.

It is not that I am opposed to rehabilitation. Who, for heaven's sake, *could* be against rehabilitation? I do have a strong reservation, however, about the nature of rehabilitation. To turn a vicious killer into some sort of celebrity in newspaper columns and on television and radio is not my idea of rehabilitation. The fact that a killer hasn't committed a crime while under round-the-clock surveillance in prison is not proof, to me, of rehabilitation.

The fact that a murderer has donated blood to the Red Cross or written a book—a common project among law-abiding citizens—is not a sure indication, to me, that he is ready to return to society.

I do not take pleasure in the execution of a human being. I would not be at all opposed to a convicted killer's being put to constructive work—possibly for life—with every nickel of his earnings used as some sort of restitution to his victim's survivors. Why do the bleeding hearts find such ideas repulsive? But the sight of a murderer (I refer now to brutal, premeditated killings for monetary gain or sexual satisfaction) lounging in his cell like a VIP, puffing on a cigar while being fawned on by newsmen (as happened in Chicago recently) makes me profoundly sick.

And this is not the worst. The bleeding hearts recently managed to get the law changed so that a convicted killer sentenced to life imprisonment no longer has to serve life. Parole, after a few years, is becoming easier all the time.

One last point. I would suggest that the bleeding hearts take time out—between writing letters that cry over the horror of execution and say nothing of the horror of murder—and go look up the records at the police station. Let them count the number of murders committed in Chicago in the last decade—then count the number of executions for the same period.

Having done that, they will find me in support of their favorite argument—that the death penalty does not stop murders. Of course it doesn't. It's hardly ever imposed.

●●●●●●●●●●●●●●●●●●●●●●

Isn't it time we put the lid back on the sewer?

I refer to the sleazy saga of that English call girl and her witless clientele. How long must this tawdriness be strung out by newspapers, magazines, radio, television, and show business?

This is not to suggest that sequels to the story, when they constitute actual news, should be suppressed. Especially since it involved highly placed people, this story had strong news value and deserved to be covered.

What nettles me is the sordid exploitation that followed.

Since the story broke, the prostitute involved has become an international celebrity. She has been paid handsomely for interviews in the British press. She has sold to a London weekly an indiscreet letter which she received from a British member of Parliament.

She has sold several other stories to Lord Beaverbrook's

Sunday Express. She has signed an $85,000 contract for the publication of her "memoirs" in another newspaper, *News of the World*.

She has been written up in tiresome detail, in countless magazines. She has been offered at least two movie contracts, including one from this country. She has also received an offer to "star" in a Nevada nightclub revue.

She has a firm $14,000-a-week contract (for twelve weeks) to serve as mistress of ceremonies in a London night spot. The owner of this joint airily explains the booking with this illuminating remark: "From some of the comments she has already made, this young lady obviously has a tremendous sense of humor."

Sure she has. A million laughs, this girl.

One thing is certain, she must at least be chuckling all the way to the bank. For the offers continue to pour in, to a point where she has found it necessary to incorporate herself as a business firm.

Nor are we without blame on this side of the sea. Over the weekend came news that a large daily newspaper in New York had signed a contract with the woman's former attorney. For a price not mentioned, he will try to titillate readers with his side of the affair.

These thoughts are not meant to point a scornful finger at the woman involved. What she wishes to do with her private life is of no concern here. However, some of us are sickened by the conduct of the dollar-dotty parasites who have crowded about her with nothing in mind but greedy exploitation.

And, as a newspaperman, I am frankly embarrassed by the behavior of some elements in my profession. What has happened, for heaven's sake, to the ethics of the communication media? Doesn't this smell of high hypocrisy? What sort of an example are the public podiums setting for young people, when book and magazine and newspaper publishers are stumbling over themselves to commercialize this misfortune?

I have to side with Harold Wilson, leader of the Labor opposition in the British Parliament, who said the other day: "There is something utterly nauseating about a system of society which pays a harlot 25 times as much as it pays its prime minister, and 500 times as much as it pays some of its ministers of religion."

At about the same time Lord Shawcross, who headed the Royal Commission on the Press last year, asked these questions:

"Is the publicizing of pimps, prostitutes and perverts in highly paid interviews or feature articles really a good thing? Is it wise to advertise the fact that the wages of sin are often very high?"

A more penetrating question was posed to me a few days ago. Someone asked: "What must the Communists be thinking of all this?"

The answer was both simple and terrifying. It was in their headlines: Valentina, their young cosmonette.

They were exploiting the heights to which a woman can rise. And we are still exploiting the depths to which she can tumble.

••••••••••••••••••••••

Dishonest as it is, there seems to be a certain fascination to the phony come-on in some areas of advertising.

About a century ago, a British-type Barnum made a fortune with a sleazy sideshow whose main attraction was, as the poster proclaimed: "A Four-Legged Animal with Its Tail Where Its Head Should Be!" Crowds shelled out shillings like crazy to see the strange beast which turned out to be, appropriately enough, a jackass. It was hitched backward in its stall.

More recently, the come-on has become standard on movie marquees: "A Cast Of Thousands!" (That's six thousand horses and the producer's relatives). "Two Years in the Making!" (Monumental hangovers and long meetings at the bank). Occasionally the come-on will warn that no one will be allowed in the theater during the film's final moments. I'm surprised the hucksters haven't used that gimmick on *Cleopatra.* Why not a blurb that says: "No One Will Be Seated During the Last Two Hours and 48 minutes of This Picture."

The trouble with this idea is that it could play havoc on people sneaking out to see the film on their lunch hour.

There's a great deal of come-on, too, on the covers of some paperback books. You gaze at the voluptuous redhead reclining on the Victorian bed and then you glance at the title: *Raising Gnus For Fun And Profit.*

Lately the magazines have gone all-out for the cover come-on. Once-staid publications are now so littered with story titles and exclamation points that it's sometimes hard to identify the magazine itself. And the bait is often conflicting. Here's one that tells us we now live longer, and that life begins at sixty. Next to it is another that proclaims: "The Terrifying Dead-at-Forty Toll of Heart Disease!" You can have a heart attack right there, trying to decide which one to buy.

And it's a rare magazine cover these days that doesn't have the word "cancer" on it (usually followed by three exclamation points). This ailment currently adorns almost as many covers as does Liz Taylor—a sales natural. (I can see the publisher of *Symmetrical Architecture* screaming at his editor: "Drop that story on split-levels, Bascomb, and dig up a new angle on cancer in the ranch styles.")

Once I saw a magazine that had the perfect parlay—a story about cancer among movie stars, a story about the Liz Taylor-Dick Burton ennui, and the inevitable, tasteless wordage on John Kennedy's family.

Passing up the confidential-exposé magazines, I spotted these titles side by side the other day:

"They're Whispering about Liz—Burton's Driving Her to Madness"; "I Took My Clothes Off to Become a Star"; "You're Not Modest—You're Frigid!" "Liz Tells Burton—You Must Marry Me!"; "We Played House Right Under His Mother's Nose"; "My Girl Friend Told Me It's Easier After the First Time"; "Mrs. Burton's Plan to Ruin Liz"; "Killing People Is Normal for Me"; "Carol Burnett Stole My Husband!"; "How It Feels To Act in the Nude"; "I Took A Lover Because I Love My Husband"; "Sex Below the 38th Parallel"; "My Four-Day Holiday From Morals"; and "I Had to Baby-Sit on My Wedding Night." (I was tempted to buy that last one, but it didn't fit very well inside *Harper's*).

One wonders what visitors to this country must think as they examine our newsstands.

And it appears that the worst is yet to come.

I can hear it now:

"Hey, Bascomb! Forget the cancer story and take this call from London. A Miss Keeler . . ."

••••••••••••••••••••••

Some years ago a few common cuss words like "hell" and "damn" were introduced in the movies. Some people, looking ahead a little, suggested this might not be a good idea. Not because the words were offensive (they are in fairly general use), but because they might open the door to more serious tampering.

They were not advocating censorship. They were asking for restraint, for a guideline of good taste. For this, they were labeled "bluenoses" by sophisticated critics seeking unlimited freedom of everything. Among these overly liberal critics were some who preferred to ignore the responsibilities of good taste and morality that go with freedom.

So mild words like "hell" and "damn" stayed. And, as those awful "bluenoses" predicted, the door did open, and gradually, just about everything went through—masquerading under the dishonest excuse of "realism" and "art" and "freedom of expression." The progress from "hell" and "damn" has reached a point where, in a movie now being looked at by New York's Board of Regents, the sexual act is filmed in detail in two scenes—one of them lasting eight minutes.

Another movie (filmed in Europe and currently being challenged in a New York court) deals with the homosexual behavior of a social welfare worker with his charge of juvenile delinquents (all six of whom rape a teen-age girl they've made drunk), and includes a scene of sexual bestiality (a prostitute and a dog). The same Board of Regents is having problems with still another movie (about a private girls' school) because of nude bathing scenes featuring lesbians and, as the Regents' report puts it, "two lesbians kissing passionately as they lay in bed."

Persons who have shown concern for such abuses have earned, from certain quarters, the label of "bluenose"—a term which has now passed into the language as derisive and even insulting. I am one of those who is often called a "bluenose." For four years I have been saying that the "hell and damn" tragedy of the movies would likely start corroding television in the home. For four years I got the label of "bluenose" flung at me so often my ear lobes have turned purple.

It has reached a point where the "bluenose," thanks to pressure from those who crusade for all-out freedom of expression, is supposed to feel like an outcast, a laughable pariah.

But I am gradually discovering that a lot of other people don't mind being called "bluenose." The mail shows that many fathers and mothers are so immensely concerned with this problem that they are prepared to rebel against the so-called stigma of being a "bluenose" or "square" or "party-pooper"—if stigma it is.

For that reason I am officially founding Bluenoses Inc., a non-profit organization opposed to senseless censorship, but dedicated to promoting decency and taste in the arts through the support of intelligent, creative work and the absolute shunning of movie, book, magazine and television trash. Where controls are needed—as in the case of pornography masquerading as "art"—Bluenoses Inc. will support controls.

Where opponents argue that no one can draw the line between pornography and art, Bluenoses Inc. will retort that a civilization that can transplant kidneys and put men into space can certainly differentiate between pornography and art.

Where opponents cry that controls interfere with freedom, Bluenoses Inc. will point to traffic stop signs, which, after all, interfere with one's freedom of movement. Where they whine that controls destroy man's free access to his needs and wants, Bluenoses Inc. will point to the controls that keep a child from buying cigarettes and keep an adult from buying certain drugs without a prescription—neither of which has stalled man's pursuit of happiness.

The motto of Bluenoses Inc. will be: "Hit Them Where It Hurts—in the Pocketbook." Its members will bear the badge of "bluenose" with honor and pride. The days of embarrassment and humiliation are over.

Bluenoses Inc. will have no dues nor meetings—simply a common bond holding them together in the knowledge that one need not be ashamed to stand up for what he believes.

The only cost of membership is a five-cent stamp on a letter or card signifying a desire to join.

••••••••••••••••••••••

In its review of a current novel, *Time* Magazine says that in its effort to be a satire the book "ends up dirty as hell." Then the magazine adds:

"No reviewer has said so. It seems that there is hardly a literary critic on earth today who would risk seeming a prude in print."

Maybe so. But this sad trait does not apply to an awful lot of laymen—ordinary citizens who are fed up to the teeth with the sickening vulgarizing of the arts, notably the stage, the screen, books, and television. I have just had this brought home to me in dramatic fashion.

A few weeks ago this column concerned itself with the insulting, derisive use of the term "bluenose." This is the label with which certain sophisticates have tagged anyone who has shown concern for the disgraceful abuses in the arts today. For just too long, now, a certain coterie of "intellectuals" have flung the epithet "bluenose" at anyone who has dared plead for restraint, good taste, and decency. Their thesis: Anyone who sees filth in a book or play or movie has a filthy mind.

This is a malicious untruth, and I suggested it was time

it be nailed for the shabby lie that it is. I also said that, thanks to pressure from those who crusade for all-out "freedom of expression" (and forget the responsibilities that go with that freedom), the "bluenose" was supposed to feel like a miserable outcast.

As one who has been roundly assailed by these campaigners for "realism" (which is often slime masquerading as art), I came out four-square as a "bluenose" and founded a non-profit, no-dues organization called Bluenoses Inc. I wondered if any readers cared to join.

Frankly, I expected about fifty or sixty answers, since I was asking readers to ally themselves with an unpopular cause, one that is sometimes a social embarrassment.

The number of those who have joined Bluenoses Inc. is now at five thousand, and each mail delivery brings a new batch of members. Some sent telegrams, some joined by phone (these are not counted in the total). The number of letters and their contents have been truly astounding. They come from college students, business executives, wives, mothers, servicemen, professional people, government officials, and a few members of the clergy.

It was amazing to find so many of these letters written by men who made it clear they were anything but prudes. But they also made clear their disgust with the evils that so-called "creative freedom" has wrought.

Some readers offered to send money to set up Bluenoses Inc. as a national organization with a paid staff (no money is being accepted). Others offered to donate office help. Others offered to donate several hours a week as unpaid workers. Many said they would be delighted to pay lifetime dues. Still others offered to pay for full-page advertisements in their neighborhood newspapers ("Long Live Bluenoses Inc.!").

Many letters included as many as twenty-five and thirty names of neighbors and friends of the letter-writer who were applying for membership in groups. In several instances the entire membership of women's and civic clubs "signed in" as members of Bluenoses Inc. In other cases, readers said they had even telephoned their relatives in other cities to urge them to join up.

Some readers sent in drawings for proposed Bluenose Inc. badges. Hundreds of letters closed with variations on this line: "We will be glad to disregard the ridicule and wear the Bluenoses Inc. label as a badge of honor."

Countless readers wrote: "At last we have a spokesman in the press." In almost all instances this message was stressed: "We're behind you. Stay with it!" Only four dissenting letters were received.

The point of this report on Bluenoses Inc. is that the response makes it clear that such an organization is needed in this country. It shows that there is not as much complacency among the "little people" in this country as we are led to believe there is. It shows plainly that the people care, providing they know they are not alone and especially when the call comes from a mass medium of communication —the newspaper.

••••••••••••••••••••••

Many among the thousands who have joined my new organization, Bluenoses Inc., are asking what they can do about the morons who are out to corrupt the arts. Here's one example of the several things that can be done. It comes from a Weirton, West Virginia, woman, one of the early Bluenose joiners.

What she did was get up from her chair, quit thinking about the ugly situation, and *do* something about it. In this case it dealt with boorish commercials being screamed out by one of those big-mouth, tiny-brain disk jockeys who infest so many radio stations. The program in question, aired nightly, was aimed directly at teen-agers and the commercial was for a driving range. Here's one of these babblings, as recorded on tape:

"Hey, listen, I want to talk to all you studs out there. You tired of always doing the same things on dates . . . you know, never anything new or different? I always hear the same complaints—this town is dead, man. Never anything to do. Well, I've got a quick solution.

"You hop in your mobile, get your chicken, zip out there to ——— Driving Range. They got all kinds of crazy pits out there, like the miniature golf course—you know, where you can test with your girl for the—heh, heh—putting irons. Yeah. And if you're steamed up, head over to the driving range and bang out a couple of those 200-yarders. Or show what a super stud you were in Little League by trying out the new batting cages . . . Any way you cut the mustard, it's going to be an exciting evening. Then when you take your honey home and—heh, heh—you know, walk her to the door, and she'll get that—heh, heh—certain look in her eye, and she'll say: 'Honey, you didn't quite make it, but, boy, that ——— Driving Range sure did.' Yeah!"

The clod's other mouthing went like this: "Listen, some night some of you studs might want to show your honey what a winner you are. Only one place to go, the ——— Driving Range. Once there, you know, flex a little bit and then—heh, heh—head over to the range. If you're really energetic you can aim at the kid who's picking up the balls—

heh, heh. No special prizes, but at any rate you can have a ball. Then in case you have a little argument over the length of your last drive, head over to that archery course and place your honey directly in front of those moving or stationary targets and just fire away. Then, if she's still giving you a little gas, make it over to the batting cages. Then, when you drag your honey to the car, slightly wounded and completely exhausted, it's up to you from there. Anyway, you can thank the ——— Driving Range. It makes it."

These commercials crashed through the air for two weeks, and finally the West Virginia lady, incensed that this sort of flip vulgarity was directed specifically to youngsters on dates, decided to go into action. She went right to the top and, after some research and calls, was able to contact the president of the corporation that owned the station. The president, apparently unaware of what was going on at his station, promptly fired the disk jockey.

Often it's better to pass up the underlings and go directly to the boss. When a Chicago station recently changed from its long-standing "good music" policy to a raucous rock-'n'-roll format, a nun called the station to inquire as to what was happening. The nun tells me that she identified herself as the superior of a convent in the Chicago area. A wise-guy type at the other end of the line rewarded her concern with: "What's the matter? Don't you like the twist?"

What is admirable about the West Virginia woman is that she troubled herself—and there's a physical effort involved—to follow through. The first easy way is to get angry and do nothing. The next easy way is to get angry and just talk about it. The third easy way is to get angry and complain to some switchboard operator. But the real way is to go to the top.

This, of course, touches upon the motto of Bluenoses Inc., which is: "Hit Them Where It Hurts—in the Pocketbook."

••••••••••••••••••••

There is one aspect of the topless swimming suit controversy that has hardly been mentioned. That is the impact that all this nonsense must have on youth, especially teen-agers.

In the last decade, teen-agers have taken their lumps. They've been called silly and rebellious, and the relative handful that flouts the law creates ugly publicity that hurts the decent majority. Further, a bad (and unfair) image of the American teen-ager has been carried abroad by sordid movies, television, and books spawned in intellectual sewers. Sadly, the good things that teen-agers do seldom intrude on that image.

We adults sneer at the youngsters because they enjoy, say, the Beatles, and we say: "What are the kids coming to?" I admit that once or twice I made remarks about the Beatle thing that were uncomplimentary to teen-agers. At this point I take it back and apologize to the kids.

I do so because the teen-agers have the adults in an embarrassing spot. For the dollar-grubbing element among adults is currently advocating the baring of female breasts in public. Among this group, the sight of a young woman preening herself in the semi-nude on a public beach, or toiling in the semi-nude as a restaurant waitress is considered "chic" and "stylish," and to think otherwise is to be a bluenose who looks on the human figure as something dirty.

The chic-and-stylish faction refuses to understand that those who are for modesty are not against female beauty or modern styles, but simply suggest that what is acceptable in the privacy of the home is not necessarily so in public.

Be that as it may, it's quite in order for teen-agers to observe these nuisances—from oldsters who should be setting an example—and ask: "What are adults coming to?" For when we adults behave in this fashion, we are nothing but hypocrites.

Fortunately, the vast majority of teen-agers are endowed with common sense. One can think of many examples, but I'll just cite one: The Modesty Crusade.

Modesty Crusade consists of youngsters who not only have common sense, they actually set an example for less endowed adults. It was formed by teen-agers to promote modesty and good taste in girls' clothing. Its secondary goal is to create a demand for stylishly modest clothing so that manufacturers will supply it.

It was started by a group of high school girls in Cincinnati more than sixteen years ago. In 1951, standards of decency and style were established at a Chicago meeting and the movement fell under sponsorship of Chicago Inter-Student Catholic Action. It flourishes in every state of the union as well as Puerto Rico, Trinidad, and the Philippines.

Every winter Modesty Crusade stages a fashion show at a large Chicago hotel usually attended by about 3000 people. The next one will be held four months from now and already 1200 girls from Catholic high schools have announced they will try out for it.

At one of the fashion shows a few years back, the late Albert Cardinal Meyer said:

"We do not look upon such organizations as pressure groups to impose upon others a moral code which these others do not accept. We look upon them as associations of our own, determined through united action to be willing courageously to set an example in defense of traditional standards . . . organizations for teen-agers who are unwilling to sit idly by while the evil spirit of immodesty goes about brazenly seeking whom it may devour."

What's more, modesty is feminine. And everybody loves feminine women. Even bluenoses.

●●●●●●●●●●●●●●●●●●●●●●

A little mound of mail has been piling up on my desk asking why I haven't dedicated at least part of a column to the presidential election campaign and its candidates. The theme of these letters—from both Democrats and Republicans—runs along this line: "Isn't there something in the campaign which would move you to comment?"

Well, since I've been asked, there is something which has moved me in this, a campaign which has seen low blows struck by both sides. I refer to a "psychiatric survey" of Barry Goldwater instituted by one Ralph Ginsburg.

Now, broadly speaking, a sadistic exercise like this one would likely have gone almost unnoticed except for two reasons: First, by the nature of their profession, psychiatrists attract a great deal of public notice when they pronounce a judgment—whether it deals with the alleged reasons behind the racial crisis or the suspicious motives in the mind of a man who starts his day by lacing his right shoe before his left.

The other reason is that Ginsburg, sadly, is a controversial man and controversial men do have a way of crawling into the headlines.

Ginsburg is best known as a publisher of erotic magazines, one of which has earned him a five-year prison term and a $42,000 fine.

Last month, Ginsburg addressed a questionnaire to the psychiatrists on the roster of the American Medical Association. The central question was loaded for Barry. It asked: "Is Barry Goldwater psychologically fit to be President of the United States?"

More shocking than the question itself, I feel, was the fact that 14 per cent of the psychiatrists to whom the questionnaire was addressed had no qualms about answering it —despite the fact that they did not know Goldwater and based their judgment only on seeing the man on television or reading about him in the press. Of this total, 1189 pronounced Goldwater unfit while 675 declared him fit.

I don't know about you, but it makes me wonder about a profession into whose hands men and women sometimes place their lives.

For example, the supervising psychiatrist of a New York hospital concluded that "it is abundantly clear to me that Goldwater never forgave his father for being a Jew." One Los Angeles psychiatrist wrote: "From television appearances it is clear that Goldwater hates and fears his wife."

A San Francisco psychiatrist answered this way: "Consistent with Goldwater's paranoid traits is his sensitivity to questions about his honesty and integrity—obvious unconscious substitutes for his masculinity. I have the feeling that if someone were to question Goldwater about his masculinity in those terms, the candidate would lose control of himself."

A Stamford, Connecticut, psychiatrist said that Goldwater "consciously wants to destroy the world with atomic bombs" and added that any doctor "who does not agree with the above is himself psychologically unfit to be a psychiatrist."

There was quite a number of other judgments, pronounced by supposedly wise men who based their opinion on the sight of the man on television. The whole thing is too disgusting to belabor here, but what a commentary on the art of the smear.

I spoke about this affair with Dr. H. M. Visotsky, Director of the Department of Mental Health for the State of Illinois. "What this did," he said, "was to hurt the image of psychiatry and the mental health movement. Psychiatrists, as other citizens, have a right to opinions but these should not be incorporated in the campaign. Such judgments should require a personal examination of the subject as well as an evaluation of his personal and medical history. It's unfortunate for the profession that some psychiatrists felt impelled to give personal opinions that could be construed as professional.

"Yes, I got the questionnaire. I threw it in the wastebasket."

••••••••••••••••••••••

At about three o'clock of a recent morning, a young woman, manager of a tavern, was stabbed to death as she neared her home after work in New York City. Her cries reportedly aroused from their sleep thirty-eight persons, who either saw or heard part of the attack. Twice their voices and the turning on of their lights scared the killer away; twice he returned to finish the grisly job.

Of the thirty-eight "witnesses"—under the conditions, this is not an accurate term—only one called the police.

Officials of the New York police department have termed the mass apathy as brutal callousness, a shocking outrage. The incident created quite a to-do on television and in the press. A performer on one of those so-called "satire" programs looked sternly into the camera and rasped: "We hope you (the victim's neighbors) sleep soundly tonight." A pall of shame has been dropped on these people—some of whom apparently did not want to become "involved."

I can't join the chorus of condemnation.

To begin with, not all of these people should be scorned for shunning involvement. It's entirely credible that some individuals, aroused from sleep at that hour, are not fully conscious nor aware of the nature of the noises that awakened them (some "witnesses" thought it was a lovers' quarrel).

For the rest, there is reason to understand their fear of becoming involved, though it can hardly be condoned.

Some police departments voice shock when a tragedy such as this one occurs, lashing it as shabby citizenship. But the fact is that in many instances people who come forward as good citizens are rewarded with pretty shabby treatment themselves. One dramatic instance was the fate of the young man who, in New York a few years ago, spotted the notorious bank robber and escape artist, Willie Sutton, and went to the police. Sutton was captured and the young man was hailed as a "good citizen."

But some Bigmouth in the police department blabbed the whole thing publicly, and the young man's name, address, place of work, and other details were printed in the newspapers. A month later he was murdered in the streets. His killers were never found. He had become another dead hero.

More recently in Chicago, the car of an associate of hoodlums was bombed in front of the Criminal Courts building. A witness to the attempted assassination came forward, like a "good citizen." In no time at all another Bigmouth in one of our law-enforcement agencies blabbed again and soon the witness, and members of his family, were receiving threatening phone calls from the cowardly morons who indulge in such things. The witness and his family had to be spirited out of the city.

In countless instances, witnesses who felt they were doing their duty have found themselves enmeshed in a troublesome net of frustration. They have had to return to court time and time again while attorneys for the defense and prosecution acquired delay after delay for weeks, months and even years. The cost to these "good citizens" in wasted time and personal discomfort, at the whims of judges who couldn't care less, cannot be estimated. I have received many letters from such frustrated witnesses recounting the misery their good citizenship brought them, most winding up with: "Never again."

It is possible to understand the reluctance of some to come forward. In too many cases they do not get the privacy and protection they deserve, and suffer from the lack of discretion shown by newspapers, radio, and television.

For these reasons the treatment given the incident by that television program was sad. The program holds claim to be a satire, but it simply descended into cruelty.

Before bellowing their wrath on the sleeping New Yorkers who did nothing, the performers should have asked themselves the question each citizen should ask himself:

What would I have done?

••••••••••••••••••••••

There will be a certain amount of displeasure in many a home today as a result of television's hour-by-hour coverage of Pope Paul VI's visit to New York City.

It marked the first time that the spiritual head of the Roman Catholic Church has ever come to America, and the networks went all-out to follow his stay in Manhattan.

Only twice before have the networks blacked out all entertainment programs—during the funeral ceremonies of Presidents Roosevelt (radio) and Kennedy (radio and television).

There will be objections, expectedly, from some television fans who feel that a visit here from the head of one religious denomination is not of sufficient importance to warrant total suspension of the regular schedule. But the networks felt otherwise.

It is possible to sympathize with those who object. There is no question that the Pope's journey to New York was a news event of monumental importance. But it is also possible to wonder if the networks should have delivered the same exact coverage simultaneously. There is no denying that such coverage represented a respect for public service responsibility on the part of the medium, and this is commendable. At the same time one wonders why the medium could not come up with a system of coverage that would have permitted one or two of the three networks to carry on with normal programing while a news occurrence such as this one was being properly covered on living room screens.

Perhaps the networks could take turns handling news happenings of stature (such as the space shots) so some portions of the regular schedule are not blacked out and the news event itself is available on at least one station for those who wish it in total coverage.

It should be faced—and it is not irreverent to face it—that the visit of the Pope was not of major importance to substantial segments of the population. Perhaps the answer might have been to telecast only the highlights of such events, as against uninterrupted, minute-by-minute coverage.

If newspapers were to give up their entire editions to one

news event—dropping such "regular schedule" features as the comics, the crossword puzzle, the sports section and so on—there would be widespread protest. And the protest would be understandable.

Similarly, there will be protests from television viewers over the papal coverage. I am not that fond of the daytime soap operas or nighttime's Lucille Ball, Jesse James, Ben Casey, and Hazel that I will be among the protesters. But I recognize the reasons for the protests and the rights of the protesters.

Certainly there is a solution to this problem, and the networks should apply themselves to it collectively.

The suggestion, incidentally, comes from one who is rather fond of Pope Paul—as most Catholics are.

•••••••••••••••••••••

On a recent afternoon a young man showed up as a solitary picket in front of the White House. He carried a sign that said: "Rent A Protest Marcher, $2 An Hour."

There is some humor in this incident, though it is far from being really funny. For it points up the abuses that have seemingly been allowed to creep into this pastime of picketing. Countless citizens are being inconvenienced by irresponsible dunderheads who flout the laws, and nothing seems to happen. Traffic is brought to a standstill at the whim of certain groups that seem to enjoy some special immunity. The lives of policemen are placed in jeopardy (you never know when a bird-brain will become a hothead and fling a brick), but that doesn't seem to bother some segments of our courts.

What in the name of common sense is going on around the country?

Last month, dozens of bleeding hearts protesting our Vietnam policies sat down in the middle of the Midwest's busiest intersection, State and Madison streets in Chicago's Loop. Their leader shouted instructions to halt as much traffic as possible, after the mob had failed to crash into the Federal Building. Forty of them were carried away to the police station.

More recently, hundreds of noisy demonstrators went at it again during the Chicago hearings of the House Un-American Activities Committee. They included young mothers unaverse to risking the lives of their babies whom they carried in their arms or in buggies. They included a cigar-chomping female beatnik, and they refused to leave the hearing room which had been ordered cleared by federal authorities.

Some of them bolted through police lines and threw themselves under police cars, including moving police cars. When they were removed, for reasons of public safety, their supporters whined about "police brutality."

A little while back, hundreds of so-called "civil rights workers" managed to bring most Loop traffic to a halt at the evening rush hour. I say "so-called" because the public respects decent, sincere civil rights workers but most of the characters I'm referring to are not civil rights workers. They are bums who have a way of subsisting without having to go to work.

Ignoring a court order to clear a courtroom is a crime. So is kicking a policeman. So is halting traffic. So is flinging one's body under moving police cars. So is crashing through police lines set up for the public's safety.

All these things are crimes, yet they go on all the time in Chicago and in many parts of the nation. Then why no punishment? Are the extremists among civil rights workers above the law? Does being unhappy about the law as constituted give one the right to break it?

It happens that lots of people don't like, for example, the personal property tax. But it is a law. How far would they get if they decided to protest it by halting Loop traffic or performing a "sit-in" at a government building?

What would happen if I decided to keep my children out of school, as is done in Chicago by some "civil rights workers?" I'd have a truant officer on my tail.

Yet we've been warned that next week there will be another—the third—school boycott in Chicago. During the last one the "civil rights leaders" who brought it about were told that they would be prosecuted. What happened? Nothing.

A few weeks ago an Alabama lieutenant of Martin Luther King, himself a cleric, warned: "We're coming up to Chicago to create confusion and disturb the peace. We're going to close Chicago down, get the rules straight, and then open it up again."

I may be dense, but this sounds to me like anarchy and inciting to riot. Is that, too, a crime for thee but not for me?

••••••••••••••••••••••

"Can you find it in you," the voice on the phone said, "to say something good about the man who killed himself for Vietnam?"

The reference was to the thirty-one-year-old man who turned himself into a human torch earlier this month in Washington. Since then there have been two incidents of a similar nature. A twenty-two-year-old member of a pacifist organization doused himself with kerosene, set a match to his body, and went up in a sheet of flame. He died thirty-three hours later.

While her husband was inside the house watching television, a twenty-four-year-old South Bend, Indiana, woman set herself on fire in the front yard. She has since recovered.

Apparently the two suicides and the attempted suicide were committed as dramatic public protests against our involvement in Vietnam.

In the case of the man who burned himself to death in Washington, his widow said the next day:

"He has given his life to express his concern over the great loss of life and human suffering caused by the war in Vietnam. He was protesting our government's deep military involvement in this war."

Originally he had planned to inflict the same grotesque death on his one-year-old daughter. He had her in his arms when he set himself afire, but was persuaded by horrified passers-by to drop her. He left a widow and three children.

The twenty-two-year-old who immolated himself in front of the United Nations building said on his deathbed: "I want to live."

The South Bend woman, mother of two small children, said: "All the world's problems are my problems." A third child, three months old, had suffocated in her crib just recently, and the husband suggested this tragedy had deeply disturbed his wife.

What can one say about people who set themselves on fire to protest war—if that is indeed the real reason for the suicide?

One can only express sorrow at the tragedy, not only because the deaths are needless but because they are fruitless. I find it difficult to equate self-destruction with martyrdom.

Further, one cannot be certain of the deeply intimate motives for suicide. Is it Vietnam, or is it something else? (Since these incidents, a young woman killed herself in the same way but shortly before dying gave an ill-starred love affair as the reason.)

But if it is Vietnam, how sad and futile that a person should take such means to protest the policies of one's government. A man who wishes to fight what he considers an injustice does his cause no good when he is dead. His voice is useless if he is silent.

It may be that a "conscience" is needed to continuously remind us that war is inhuman, though I certainly don't accept those unwashed, unshaved slug-a-bed sign carriers as any sort of conscience. It would seem that the two men who chose self-immolation could have been a louder, clearer, more effective "conscience" if they had used the usual, accepted forms of protest.

As it is, they made headlines. They left behind them loved ones, especially little children who need them. Now they are dead and their usefulness as a "conscience" is at an end.

I feel sorrow for the bereaved. But the dead taught me nothing that I did not know.

Reflections while waiting for the set to warm up

Some television writers sigh that all the good plots—especially the seven principal story-lines on which all fiction is supposedly based—have been used up. Nonsense. Many good story-lines have yet to be used. It's time the following were tried out:

For hours, the lovesick girl has been on the window ledge, threatening to jump. In vain the police and her family have tried to coax her off her perch. Finally the man who jilted her volunteers to bring her in. But the poor fellow misses his footing and plunges below. She watches him fall, mutters: "This is ridiculous," and scoots in to safety.

Safari Pithelmet pushes on through the dense jungle, convinced that there *is* a white goddess ruling a savage tribe just beyond the next mountain. He finds her, at last, serenely nibbling on cocoa leaves. She's seventy-eight, toothless, totally bald, and she cackles: "What took you so long, dearie?"

The once famous surgeon is now a drunken derelict, sodden by years of cheap wine. One night he stumbles upon a train wreck. Among the seriously injured is a prince from Cambodia who can be saved by immediate surgery. The doctor calls for boiling water, but there's no water for miles around. Somebody asks if a bottle of whiskey will do. The doctor says yes, and, needing something to calm his hungover nerves, takes a long, soulful swig and promptly passes out.

At the age of seven, Horatio Algernon is supporting his widowed mother by selling newspapers. Later he takes to shining shoes and mowing lawns and earns enough to open a hot-dog stand. With profits from this he puts himself through night school and gets a degree in accountancy and a job at the bank. From assistant teller he rises in twenty-seven years to vice-president. One day, when nobody is looking, he puts $147,000 in his pocket and flies to Brazil—leaving his mother behind to reopen the hot-dog stand.

For seventeen years, Aria McTonsils has been understudy to the stars at the Metropolitan Opera, with nary a chance to be heard. One day the lead in *Carmen* breaks a leg, and Aria has her big chance. An hour before the curtain, the stagehands call a strike and the opera house is closed down. Aria McTonsils goes home to Hangnail, Arkansas, and becomes a pin-spotter in a bowling alley.

Humphrey Durancevile, serving a life term, is holed up in the jute mill with five rifles and a determination to break out. The warden's pleas are to no avail. Finally, the prison chaplain goes in alone. "Give me the gun, Durancevile," says the padre gently. "One more step," snarls Durancevile, "and I'll blow your head off!" The chaplain scoots out and tells the warden: "I think that idiot means it."

The doctor had told Murgatroid Hapless he had but six months to live; his kidneys are gone. Two months before the end he receives a phone call from the doctor advising him there had been a switch in medical reports. "We've just found your report," says the doctor excitedly, "and your kidneys are all right." Hapless is ecstatic: "Then I'll live? Oh, thank you, doctor!" The doctor says: "No, your kidneys are fine but your lungs are all shot. I give you five weeks."

Little Epsilon is broken-hearted because his dog, Spotty,

has been missing a long time. His father promises Spotty will find his way home some day. But Spotty is in the next state, where he has found a home with a nice old couple who feed him twice, not once, a day. Also, there are no children there. Spotty has always hated children.

Home from college, Claude Harvard learns his father, a civic leader, has been embezzling for years. "How about cutting me in, Pop?" he asks.

Prince Charming marries Detesta and they live miserably for years. He's always on the road, looking for rescuable damsels, and she's a terrible cook. They are divorced, and live happily ever after.

••••••••••••••••••••••

Whenever I'm looking for news in the television world and I call CBS in New York, the girl on the line will chirp: "This is CBS—the Columbia Broadcasting System." Yesterday it was different. "This is CBS," she said, "the Columbia Baseball System." The network's purchase of the New York Yankees has changed things.

I asked for William Paley, CBS's chairman of the board. "He's in Baltimore," she trilled. "We're playing the Orioles today."

How about Frank Stanton, the president? "He's locked up in his office with a stack of bubble-gum cards," she said, "and I've got orders not to disturb him."

"Bubble-gum cards?"

"The ones with the players' records on the back."

Michael Dann, the program chief, was out of town, too, so I settled for one of the network's seventy-nine vice presidents whose name escapes me. He had been listening to the ball game on radio and was miffed by the interruption. "I'm looking for news," I said.

"Orioles 4, CBS 2," he said, "but we've got a rally going."

He explained that Dann was scouting a minor-league player in Atlanta who could switch-hit and also ride a horse. "We figure he might make second base or 'Gunsmoke,'" he giggled. "Maybe both."

"Tell me about next season," I said.

"Well, Walter Cronkite's usually free in the daytime, and we're weak in the outfield so—"

"No, I mean your programs."

"Oh, that. Well, we're toying with new formats with a baseball theme. We're keen on one called 'Ben Casey at the Bat,' and there's a peachy possibility in 'Tales of Wells Fungo.'"

"Anything else?"

"We have a panel show called 'People Are Fanning' that shows promise, and we're thinking of Richard Boone for 'Have Run, Will Travel.' We've got sponsor interest in one called 'San Francisco Beats', and Mr. Stanton is high on one called 'Playball 90.'"

"Sounds familiar."

"Indeed. We want to keep the chemistry of baseball and television together. That's why we're changing 'Rawhide' to 'Horsehide,' and we're asking Rod Serling to change the title of his 'Twilight Zone' to 'Twilight Doubleheader.' Doesn't that chill you?"

"Well, I—"

"Then how's this for a scoop: 'Person to Person' is coming back under the new name of 'Piersall to Piersall.'"

"Isn't it a bit odd, a network buying into baseball?"

"What's odd? Bob Hope owns a piece of the Cleveland Indians, and he's with NBC. Bing Crosby owns a piece of the Pittsburgh Pirates, and he's with ABC. Maybe you ought to look into that."

"I understand there could be some lawsuits."

"Let 'em sue. We've got Perry Mason. And The Defenders."

"What are your chances for the pennant?"

"Don't like that word pennant, baby. Over here we're calling it Emmy."

"Okay. Where will Emmy fly this fall? Baltimore, Chicago, or at CBS—uh, Yankee Stadium?"

"Well, Yogi Bear tells me—"

"Yogi who?"

"Sorry, I keep thinking of the opposition. Yogi Berra feels confident. But he needs help on the coaching line, so we're bringing in Jackie Gleason as first-base coach, and Red Skelton will coach at third."

"But they're comedians!"

"So? Did comedy hurt the Mets? Those clowns have stolen our crowds."

"If you take the flag, won't you feel put out that your competitor, NBC, will be telecasting the World Series?"

"Not at all. We've got a master stroke. You know where the numbers are on the players' backs? Well, we're ripping them off and stitching on the big CBS eye. Doll, that's just got to grab you!"

••••••••••••••••••••••

Watching the Democratic National Convention in Atlantic City on television with a gaggle of little girls:

"What are they doing now, Daddy?"

"Well, some of the people can't get in the hall."

"Why?"

"The people inside won't let them in."

"But you said it was like a big party and they're all friends."

"Don't talk so much, dear. Daddy has to work."

"Oh, I know what happened! They came to the party, see, and they didn't bring any presents and–"

"No, it's not like that."

"Remember when Irene came to my party and I saw she don't got a present and I slammed the door and–"

"Forget that! You behaved terribly that day."

"Well, the big people do it."

"I suppose they do sometimes, dear."

"The people that can't come in–where do they come from, Daddy?"

"Mississippi."

"What's that?"

"Look at the map over there. Mississippi . . . Alabama . . . Georgia."

"But Georgia's baby-sitting."

"Not *our* Georgia. *That* Georgia."

"Who's that talking, Daddy? Look at his Adam's apple going up and down."

"That's a reporter."

"He looks hungry."

"Everybody looks hungry. They've been working very hard, and they haven't time to eat."

"And who's that?"

"His name's Hubert Humphrey."

"He doesn't look hungry, Daddy."

"Oh, he's hungry all right."

"He looks a little fat."

"I don't mean that. He's hungry for the nomina–– never mind, you wouldn't understand."

"That man making the speech, Daddy, he keeps saying to the people to come join the party. What's he say that for if they won't let their friends in?"

"Some day, when you're older—"

"Who's that, Daddy?"

"That's another reporter."

"Why's he wearing earmuffs? Is it cold out there?"

"Those are earphones and yes, I suppose it is a little cold out there right now . . ."

"Look, he's standing on somebody's shoulders and they're pushing and yelling. It's like the party you had last week—remember when you were standing on your head and you fell and—"

"KEEP QUIET! Just forget about that party. You were supposed to be in bed!"

"Look! There's the people that can't get in again. Why don't they go in the water and swim and fish, instead of trying to get in?"

"Some of them will go fishing later, I think."

"When?"

"Probably next November."

"Daddy, the people that can't get in the party—they're all black. Is that why?"

"That's part of the reason."

"When I have my parties, Daddy, there's never any black kids come. Why?"

"They don't live around here."

"Why?"

"Never mind, dear. It's like I said—some day, when you're older . . ."

•••••••••••••••••••••

Those people you see in the commercials these days—do they really exist? Where are they? Does anybody know them?

I refer to the strange people who populate the sponsor's message. Are they for real?

I wonder if wives really meet their husbands at the door when they return from work and shriek: "Honey! I've just discovered the most effective new cleanser!" And I wonder if the husbands really put down their brief case or lunch pail and dance over to the sink to watch the action. Are there such people?

My stomach's been turning over almost nightly as I watch those odd women who make a career of sniffing their friends and suggesting they switch deodorants. I mean—do women actually tell one another they can't attend that party tonight because they've got heebie-jeebies in the armpits? I recall one touching scene in a locker room where a golfer offers his deodorant to a pal who considers himself an incurable stinker. Good grief, I wouldn't let my son use my deodorant. Nor would I use his.

One biddy who bothers me is the one who carries her husband's suits to the cleaners and tells a complete stranger at the counter: "I don't know what I'll do about my husband's dandruff." And all the while she's flicking the nasty specks off his clothes. If I had dandruff and my wife told strangers about it, I'd be writing this column from Reno.

Surely you've seen the clothesline scene where one woman tells a neighbor her clothes (the neighbor's) aren't coming off whitey-white-white, and why doesn't she use *this* detergent? In my circle I venture that if one woman criticized another's washing, she'd be rewarded with a bundle of soggy linen right in the mouth. Splat!

Another routine that grates me is that bit in the supermarket when two women bump carts in the aisle. One peeks into the other's groceries and exclaims something like: "Goodness, are you still using *that* brand of soup (or juice or whatever)? Haven't you heard of *this* brand?"

I saw one recently wherein a woman accosted a male shopper pushing his cart and actually chided him for bringing home the "wrong" bathroom tissue.

And how do the accosted react? They practically kiss Old Snooper's hand and utter the equivalent of: "Bless you, you darling, for introducing me to this new *improved* whatever-it-is."

If I were shopping and some woman started pawing my groceries or inquiring about bathroom tissue I would:

1. Immediately run her down with my cart.
2. Have her arrested for disorderly conduct.
3. Start a whispering campaign about her mental stability.

Still, perhaps we shouldn't complain too much because the acting in these things is something to behold. Fewer sponsors now hire a salesman to tell you about their product. The vogue is to build an abbreviated melodrama around the product—a sort of instant theater—and clamp a grabber on your purse and heart at the same time. If they had awards for such dramatic fare I suppose the headache people would run away with most of the trophies.

Surely you recall that magnificent scene where the father returns from work to find the kids' wagons and bikes in the driveway. After much shouting and waving of arms he prepares to kick the child beneath the chin when his wife runs out with a tablet or a fizz thing. In seconds the father realizes he's been a beast and, headache gone, serenity returns to the home.

(I tried that bit once. Screamed and shrieked, took a tablet, and felt so bad about scaring the kids I offered to take them for a spin around the block. Backing out of the driveway—KRUNCHHHH!! Demolished $218 worth of bikes, wagons, buggies, and a carton containing four white mice.)

Another role with meat in it is that of the middle-aged

wife whose husband ignores her on the dance floor until she starts tinting the gray out of her hair. After that—wow! Dinner at smart clubs twice a week and twisting into dawn.

(A lady I know who used to sit home forlornly night after night was inspired by this performance. She gave herself a tint job and now she's living it up in the gay spots nightly. Her husband, though, *he* stays home and does the dishes.)

And how about the fop who offers the strange lady in a plane one of his cigarettes, and winds up with her over candlelight and wine? My insurance agent tried that once on a flight to Denver. Got sixty days as a masher.

But the dramas I enjoyed most were the ones based on cases of mistaken identity which have left the little screen. I tell you, these had suspense to warm the heart of any student of the stage. Who can forget the cigarette blurb wherein one man says to another: "Oh, I see you're a tuck-pointer?" And the other replies: "No, I'm an atomic fission physicist. I tuck-point as a hobby on weekends. Indeed, you might call me a weekend tuck-pointing atomic fission physicist."

Man, that's acting. It was the sort of emotional give-and-take that would glue me to my chair. When it was over and they'd resume with the rest of the program, *then* I'd leave for that glass of water.

••••••••••••••••••••

Television made a big liar out of me—but it paid off.

It happened earlier this month when I was asked to be one of the two impostors on "To Tell the Truth," the CBS panel game on television which stars ever-smiling, people-loving Bud Collyer.

According to producer Willie Stein, any intelligent person can be a convincing liar, and it only takes about ninety minutes of briefing. I guess I'm not intelligent because my briefing with the other impostor and the "real" character took about three hours.

That's a long time to learn how to tell a few lies with a straight face, but it was worth it. In this case, the hero of the affair was a man who had survived an exceedingly nasty plane crash in the "Black Swamp" of the Florida Everglades —three days and nights without food or protection from alligators and poisonous snakes.

The idea of the game is that the central character is sworn to tell the truth, while the two impostors each try to convince the panel that he, indeed, is coming clean while the other two are fibbing.

It sounds simple, but it can be a misery. We had to be briefed, for example, on the topography of the Everglades, its weather, the appearance and performance of various types of monoplanes and innumerable details such as the manner in which an alligator opens its mouth (all right, do YOU know?).

When you haven't been in Florida, let alone the Everglades, a show like this can be rough on the nerves. One wrong answer and you're immediately eliminated as an impostor by the panelists who know how to ask key, tricky questions. (What kind of birds, for example, would one encounter in those swamps?)

For some reason, the part that made me most nervous was the beginning, when, with my two companions, I was to stand behind a screen (only a silhouette showing) and intone the start of the show: "My name is Malcolm Jones." I had spent the previous night in the hotel room, poring over Florida maps and reading up on swamp lore and had much difficulty remembering the name of Lake Okeechobee. Seconds before the show went on the air I went over the opening line to myself—and—horrors—it kept coming out: "My name is Malcolm Okeechobee."

Stein later told me that one night one man who was supposed to say: "My name is Mickey Sullivan" goofed on his opener and, for reasons he never could explain, blurted: "My name is Mickey Spillane." You can imagine what a thing like that will do to the two other fellows standing beside him behind that screen.

In any event, I must have been a fairly good liar because panelist Peggy Cass picked me as the real item. Her reason was quaint: "He looks like he's been through a traumatic experience." In a way, Miss Cass was right; the traumatic experience was the show itself. Another panelist, Steve Rossi of the Marty Allen-Steve Rossi comedy team, also voted for me as the pilot who suffered the ordeal because, he said, "He's holding his arm as if it had been recently broken (in the crash)." I was holding it to keep it from shaking too much.

For getting two wrong votes, I and my two companions (the other impostor and the real pilot) on the program split $200.

Over the years, Stein has dug up well over 1500 liars and central characters. The most interesting one, to me, was the memory expert who failed to appear at the studio but phoned thirty minutes before air time.

"I forgot this was the day," he explained, rather mortified. "Also, at what time do you want me there?"

Oh, about the alligator's eating habits: only the bottom part of the mouth opens, the top part remains stationary.

••••••••••••••••••••••

The people who pass official judgment on commercials for the television industry seem to be obsessed with the beer and wine blurbs.

They represent the Code Authority of the National Association of Broadcasters, and they've just announced a new "interpretation" of the code, which forbids the drinking of wine and beer in commercials.

The interpretation directs that such commercials "avoid any representation of on-camera drinking as well as representations which convey the impression of excessive drinking."

In the new interpretation, the Code Authority now forbids the tilting or holding of glasses, cans and bottles close to the lips, "the wiping, smacking or pursing of lips and swallowing motion of the Adam's apple or similar actions."

What if the poor announcer smacks his lips because they happen to be chapped? What if he purses them because he can't stand the smell of the hops or the odor of grape? What if he's the nervous type who can't control his Adam's apple?

It seems to me that the Code Authority could accomplish more by going after commercials that are dishonest, or offensive (or both).

The lady swishing soap off her legs in the bathtub, for example. There is nothing repulsive about a lady's leg—quite the contrary—but a lady in the bathtub belongs in the bathroom and not in the nation's living rooms. And that goes for the girdle that won't stay up, or down or whatever it is that a girdle is supposed to do or not do.

It goes, too, for these examples of the Big Lie:

The collegian with stage fright who's unable to deliver a talk before the student body. A pal tells him to splash his hair with a certain goo before his speech, and young Tremble-Knees comes out a new Barrymore (you just know he'll make it to Congress).

The spinster type who embarks on a cruise all a-twitter about her underarm problem. A friend tells her about a certain deodorant and in the next scene the spinster type has hooked the ship's purser (all that's missing is a wedding march).

The pain-wracked grandma doubled up with arthritis. She takes a headache tablet and promptly starts swinging her grandchildren over her head (anyone for the frug?).

And do all couples have to go into a passionate Rudolph Valentino-Theda Bara embrace after one of the pair has discovered a new mouthwash or hair spray or lipstick or whatnot? The kiss is a fine social tradition, but the thirty-second open-mouth smooch is getting to be a slobbering, intrusive abuse of advertising ethics.

I'll pass up all of the above anytime for an active Adam's apple.

••••••••••••••••••••

I think I have the makings of a television series about an international spy.

He doesn't look at all like Cary Grant did in 1940. He has a pea-sized purplish wart on his left nostril.

I call him Ezekiel Schlott and he's not an unmarried charmer. He has a wife, five children, and a termitic prefab on the outskirts of town. His wife has never forgiven him for quitting his bus driver's job.

He is sixty-two years of age and about thirty pounds overweight, which accounts for his flat feet. On staircases he never dashes up three steps at a time; his blood pressure won't permit it.

He seldom uses a cigarette holder as other agents do, because his dentures are loose and it keeps sliding out of his mouth during conversation. He hates going aboard yachts, as all agents do, because he suffers from seasickness. He is as bald as a grapefruit and perspires a lot.

There's nothing wrong with his work. He's a good, loyal government man, but he has ruddy bad luck at being debonair like the other agents. On the Riviera, he doesn't saunter up to the elegant bars and order a Pernod; he rubs the top of his head with a handkerchief and asks for a beer. When the maître d' suggests pheasant under glass, he smiles nervously and wonders if he can have a hamburger.

He has never cabled his home office for another $5000. He has a $35-a-week expense account and washes his socks in the sink.

Most times, when a luscious foreign lady accosts him in the hotel lobby, he makes an excuse and goes upstairs to his room to read *U.S. News & World Report.*

If he can't escape her clutches he tries to brazen it out, but misfortune attends him. When he leans over to give her a light his lighter is invariably out of fuel, and when she sensuously blows smoke in his face, his eyes water. If she asks him to dance, he hopes the band will play "There's an Old Spinning Wheel in the Parlor."

He thinks karate is a Spanish vegetable, and twice in the last month he left his brief case in the men's room.

In emergencies, when he identifies himself to the local police department, the officers look at him and say: "Ezekiel who?"

All in all, though, Ezekiel Schlott is a good, reliable man. He smiles fairly often, and never through clenched teeth as all agents are supposed to smile. When other agents are tooling about the Côte d'Azur in their sports cars, he's playing chess by mail. He's very lonely for that pre-fab on the outskirts of town.

But he's for real. Almost.

••••••••••••••••••••••

From now on when I'm tempted to suggest that nobody watches reruns on television, I'm going to hold my tongue.

A surprising lot of people watch repeats. I speak from personal experience.

On a recent night the Chicago educational station (WTTW) repeated a "Book Beat" program on which I was host Robert Cromie's guest. It had originally been shown nine months ago when Cromie had graciously asked me aboard to talk about a novel I'd written, called *A Pennant for the Kremlin.*

The interview was going along at a merry clip—sometimes it takes me three minutes to answer a question—and Cromie was well-armed with interesting questions, the kind that lend themselves to stimulating give-and-take.

We were having such a fine time of it that evidently both Cromie and I lost track of the clock ticking away. Suddenly, Cromie shifted into a field that fascinates anyone who has ever written a book.

The bane of all authors, he explained, is the gremlin who somehow creeps into the mind of the author and causes him to commit a screaming boo-boo—an error which should never have been put to paper but, if so put, should have been caught and rectified by the publisher's editorial staff.

"Tell me," Cromie asked, "is there by a chance a howler in your book?"

Well, by chance there was a magnificent one in the book, and I was glad for the chance to explain, and perhaps minimize, it.

"Yes," I began, "there's a real crazy one in the book. You see, there's this fellow, and he—"

At this point Cromie caught a frantic signal from the floor director and sadly broke in: "I'm sorry," he said, "but I see that our time is up." The half-hour, which seemed to have started five minutes ago, was already over.

So I was left sitting there, my mouth open in mid-sentence.

The reason I know that reruns have an audience is that a startling number of viewers have phoned and written in about the cliff-hanger. Their curiosity was obviously piqued, and they want to know what the howler was. Their number includes several who read the book and missed the mistake. Here it is:

One of the characters, an important one in the book, has only one arm (the other having been shot off in the war). I went to some pains to adjust his predicament to his job—which was that of a baseball team manager.

But somewhere in the writing the gremlin struck. I had the man, in a fit of anger, flailing the heavens "with both arms."

I missed it when I checked my copy. The editors in New York missed it. The copyreaders missed it. The proofreaders missed it. Even the publisher's lawyers (who read every line with a magnifying glass) missed it. And so, obviously, did a number of readers.

Darn clever, those gremlins.

••••••••••••••••••••••

From here on in, I don't believe I will say a nasty thing about Soupy Sales.

Sales is a middle-aged gentleman who has made a career of getting splattered in the face with pies on television. I've never felt terribly uplifted by the pie-in-the-face routine, but henceforth I'll have more respect for Sales and others who use pies for laughs. It isn't easy. I got one in the kisser the other night and there's more to it than meets the eye, so to speak.

I was asked to participate in a pre-filmed slapstick segment of a program put on by the National Academy of

Television Arts and Sciences for the Emmy Award ceremonies in Chicago.

The idea was to have the host of a conversation-discussion program do a fake introduction of his guests and be assaulted by a pie in the face the moment he mentioned that one of his guests would be Soupy Sales.

Later, I was to be shown typing out a review of the event, panning the program host for pandering to low taste.

And the moment I mentioned that the program host got it in the snoot for mentioning Sales's name—SPLAAT! I got it in the snoot too.

"The thing to do," explained the director of the segment, "is to keep from blinking and pretend nothing happened."

That sounded easy, but his orders were to keep reading my fake column after the assault, suggesting I wasn't even aware that the oozy mess was all over my face.

After the pie hit—a magnificent throw by a stagehand—I couldn't see a thing.

Unfortunately I said so with an observation that doesn't lend itself to television, and the film had to be scrapped. We tried it again, and this time the view was worse than the first time. That film, too, was set aside. On the third try the stagehand aimed a little above the eyes, permitting me to read what I was supposed to read. It was a "take."

Since then, people have inquired about the pie. Was it the real thing? Was it whipped cream or ice cream? Did it hurt?

What it is, is shaving cream (the real stuff stains and smells) foamed into a paper plate. It doesn't hurt, but it does sting a bit when it spreads into the eyes. Especially when you have to read something with your eyes full of the goo.

The producer of this cinematic gem was most considerate. For one thing, he had bought me two blue shirts for the filming, and two ties. For another, he offered me a choice —regular lather or menthol. It was muggy in the studio, so I chose menthol.

Apart from the extra haberdashery, what pleases me is that the station will splice the three takes, including the two disasters, and give me the film to show during lulls at parties. If you have to show home movies, you may as well go with an epic.

And whenever I feel depressed or critical of the human race, I'll roll the film for myself. A little humility is good for everybody.

••••••••••••••••••••••

For the columnist like me whose job includes keeping an eye on television, it's that time again.

About two thirds of his friends envy his supposedly soft touch because "you get paid for just watching television." The rest express sympathy because "you have to watch that trash every night."

But this is a minor peril compared to the plight of the critic whose younger children don't quite understand what he does for a living.

When the program becomes unfit for tender eyes and ears, he orders them to go play in another room.

"But we just came from there," they'll whine. "That's three times since supper we've been in the other room."

"Then go take a bath."

"But we're not dirty! We took a bath last night."

"OK, so go outside, play with the rabbits, get dirty again, then come in and take a bath. THAT'S AN ORDER!"

I must say I have the cleanest children on the block. A bit water-logged, mind you, but white-white clean. The trouble with this system is that when it's my turn to hit the tub the hot water's all gone. So I wind up blue-blue clean.

Naturally, the sprouts want to know why they can't watch with their father.

"Because it's no good," the father explains, biting his tongue on the thought that the family that plays together stays together.

"Then why do you watch it?"

"Because I have to."

"Why?"

"Because my boss wants me to."

"Why doesn't HE watch?"

"Because that's not his job. It's my job."

"You don't sound like you like your job."

"Uh—right now, I don't."

"Then why don't you stay home, like us?"

"Because if I stay home you won't have anything to eat! Does that answer your question?"

"No. Let's eat the rabbits."

The children's favorite at my house on Sunday nights is Walt Disney, but I often turn to see what Ed Sullivan is up to at the same time. I've been switching back and forth so often that six-year-old Mark identifies this period as the Walt Sullivan show. Barbara, who's a year older, calls it the Ed Disney program.

On Thursday nights I happen to share the youngsters' affection for Woody Woodpecker, but I frequently twist to the Huntley-Brinkley Report which beams at the same hour. Once the phone rang and I heard Lisa tell the caller that I was busy watching the Huntley-Woody Report.

This constant-watching problem extends beyond the children's salad years. Two of my daughters are at the teen-age-boy-friend level, and it seems that whenever a boy comes calling I'm sprawled on a chair, eyes drowsily half closed and mouth agape—sometimes with the shoes kicked aside.

The result is that when Shonagh or Georgia says to the boy: "I'd like you to meet my father," I often suspect she doesn't *really* like me to meet him. After all, a sprawled, drowsy, shoeless father in the living room does something to the head-of-the-family image.

It makes him look like a miserable slob, that's what it does.

It isn't so bad the first time. But when this nauseating sight greets a come-a-calling boy for three weekends in a row, it's time to take drastic measures. I have taken them.

Now, when I hear the boy friend's car pull up, I tell the younger ones: "This show isn't any good. Go play in the other room."

Then I get up and join them.

New York is a nice place to visit,
but always bring an extra pair of pants

I just can't feel for the fellow who lost his heart in San Francisco. I lost my pants in New York City.

It's a dreadful experience and I bring it up only as a protest against the take-over of human activity by electronic machines. Even though we don't hear the thing clanking at our heels, we are at the age of the robot.

It happened in the forty-six-story New York Hilton Hotel, largest of the chain, which rises like a monstrous steel-and-glass wafer out of the heart of Rockefeller Center. The place is so glitteringly new that one night, in the lobby, I bypassed the ash trays and went outside on Fifty-third Street to kill my cigarette.

Since the New York Hilton can accommodate a small city, electronics has been called in to help with the work load. Remember the day when you left the morning wake-up call with the operator? The operator would coo back that she'd get you up on time and until then—sweet dreams.

Well, that old-fashioned day is gone.

What you do, at the New York Hilton, is pick up your phone and dial numerically the time you wish to be called. A recorded voice then comes on the line and asks you to speak out, between beeps, your name and room number. At this point, you yourself become a number and at the appointed time, next morning, a small blare goes off in a radio-like box on your dresser. You have to get up to shut it off, thus averting the danger of falling back on your pillow and telling the world to go you-know-where.

That same gadget on the dresser serves another purpose. Remember when you'd reach your room to find the little white message slips under your door? That's gone too. When you have a message in your box downstairs, a light flashes every three seconds from that gadget on the dresser, the machine emits a soft click-click, and the sign on the panel says: "You Have a Message." When you dial the message number on your phone, the message is read to you, and the lights and the clicking stop.

The electronic data-processing system is so frightfully fast that you can check out and pay your bill literally in ten seconds. It's quite an age in which we live.

But sometimes a machine is only human. It, too, can make a mistake.

One night my publisher had arranged an exquisite dinner downstairs in The Seven Hills, the hotel's fanciest room. It was going to be a special evening, so I sent my trousers out to be pressed—with a guarantee that I would have them back within one hour. At this point I guess I became a number again.

Two hours went by, and still no trousers. The dinner hour arrived and I became panicky, for my other suit was at the cleaners. There was, the voice on the phone said, a little problem, but my pants should be up shortly. More time passed and finally I had to send my wife downstairs to be with our host. I kept calling, and finally I got the awful truth.

"We seem," the voice on the phone said, "to have lost your pants. They've been sent to the wrong room, but we're looking for them."

It was now 8:30 P.M. "How many rooms in this hotel?" I asked.

"This hotel," the voice said (a little too proudly, I thought), "has 2153 rooms. But we'll find your pants, don't worry."

I was standing there, looking out the window at the Manhattan skyline, in my newly shined shoes, brand-new shirt, resplendent tie, smart jacket—and my shorts. The machines had made me half-naked to the world.

I wanted to cry.

Men, not machines, finally found my pants. I don't know how many rooms they searched before they found them and I'd rather not think about it. But I made the dinner. I was panting, mind you, but at least I was panted. Somebody remarked that odd things often seemed to happen to me.

Yes, I'd say that.

••••••••••••••••••••••

The other day I did something I now regret. I did it because everybody else was doing it. I'll never do it again.

I destroyed my dandelions.

Deep down—and they are deep, the little rascals—I wanted to keep them. Make what you will of this, but I think dandelions are beautiful, and yellow is such a warm, pretty color. Still, the neighbors were giving theirs the kill and giving me the eye. So I gave in.

Now the dandelions are dead, and the children are sad. They wonder where the yellow went.

It went the way of conformity, and I wish now that I had had the courage to stand my ground and let those dandelions thrive and bloom the way nature intended.

By what standard do the perfectionists call the dandelion a weed and a pest? Because it's free and populous? Because it gets along very well without human help? Because it offends the all-green monotony of the lawn? I don't accept that. The dandelion is a flower, and a vastly useful one at that. It asks nothing—not even a drop of water—and it gives so much.

You can take your roses and smell them from here to Mexicali. I'll take the dandelion anytime.

What's so great about the rose anyway? It just stands there—vain and conceited—with a look-me-over pout on its petals. Try touching it, and its thorny bushes bring blood to your hands. But you have to touch it, don't you? You must give it food and water and medicine and chemicals. You have to trim it and pamper it, and very often you have to seclude it within a fence.

Yet, with all that, it's full of diseases, and rose beetles, and chafers, and June beetles, and thrips, and Japanese beetles, and aphids (that sounds interesting, but it means lice), and other disgusting creatures. And at season's end, if it does survive, what has the rose given you? A sore back.

But the dandelion! There's a generous, loyal friend. It doesn't ask for a moment of your time, not a penny from your pocket. But its leaves make a tasty salad, and its roots can be roasted as a substitute for coffee. It has a precious, milklike liquid in its stem that has the properties of rubber (for thirty years it has been producing up to two hundred pounds of rubber per acre in Russia).

In many countries, notably France, it is a fairly common staple at mealtime. What's more, it is capable of producing a most heady wine. It serves as food for the silkworm, for which women should be grateful. And we would be hard put for honey if it weren't for what the dandelion does for the bee (or should that be vice versa?).

Even in death the supposedly lowly dandelion continues

to serve. In the nation's zoos it's a favorite luncheon for hippopotamuses, tapirs, rhinoceroses, baby giraffes, and elephants.

And who can turn from the child who walks through the door with a cluster of the umbrellalike beauties and whispers: "Here's some flowers I picked for you."

I love dandelions. Next year, I'll let them live out their short lives. For I'm on the side of the poet, J. R. Lowell, who wrote:

Dear common flower, that grow'st beside the way,
Fringing the dusty road with harmless gold,
First pledge of blithesome May,
Which children pluck and, full of pride, uphold,
High-hearted buccaneers, o'erjoyed that they
An Eldorado in the grass have found,
Which not the rich earth's ample round
May match in wealth—thou are more dear to me
Than all the prouder summer-blooms may be.

••••••••••••••••••••••

My own remembrance of Sir Winston Churchill is a deeply personal one, and the long lapse of years could never dim it.

It happened twenty years ago when, I suppose, I was more impressionable than I am now. I had been a newspaperman for just a little while, and certainly I was not yet ready for the Big Time. But fate, stirred by stubbornness, threw me into the Big Time ahead of schedule.

I had worked for a Montreal newspaper, and then been hired by United Press International. After a few months, and because I was bilingual, the news service sent me to Quebec City to open its first bureau in the French capital.

In September of that year, Mr. Churchill and President Franklin D. Roosevelt chose Quebec City as the site of their summit conference. Their host was Mackenzie King, then Prime Minister of Canada.

No need here to describe the awe of a neophyte newsman who finds himself running a news service bureau in a city where momentous history was to be made. Much of it is vague now, but I do remember that hundreds of newsmen, including the giants of the profession (William Shirer, Paul Gallico, Merriman Smith, etc.) descended on Quebec City for the event.

Because I was a beginner, so to speak, my job consisted mainly of making phone calls for the Washington press corps of UPI and writing unimportant sidebars to the main event (what time Mr. Churchill rose in the morning, what Mr. Roosevelt had for lunch and so on).

On the last day of the conference Mr. Churchill, Mr. Roosevelt, and Mr. King were to pose for official conference photographs at a site overlooking the St. Lawrence River. This was to be, also, the only "press conference" (at which the statesmen would simply read prepared statements).

It was decreed that this would be covered in a pool arrangement by just three newsmen representing the British (and Commonwealth) press, the American press, and Reuters news agency (representing the rest of the world). The hundreds of other newsmen were kept about a hundred yards away from the VIP platform.

I wanted to get up there badly. After all, the Canadian press was not directly represented, and I felt that it should be—especially by a newsman from the host city.

It happened that I knew an inspector of the Royal Canadian Mounted Police who was among those in charge of Canadian security for the event, and who worked with the Secret Service men from the United States and the men from Scotland Yard. I talked, quickly and uninterrupted, for two minutes with him, stressing the angles of local and Canadian pride. He consulted with Scotland Yard and the Secret Service and suddenly, my knees buckling a bit, I was being escorted to the platform. I had made it through sheer luck.

Mr. Roosevelt and Mr. King were already seated, and then Mr. Churchill arrived, a bit late. I was within a few feet of him, almost breathless as I awaited the first great words from the mighty man. He squinted at the bright sun glaring down on the scene, and the bulldog scowl came to his face as he literally growled:

"Must I sit here—with that damned sun in my eyes!"

There's no moral to all this except that it often made me think of Kipling's definition of a man, one who can "walk with kings, nor lose the common touch."

Mr. Churchill certainly did.

●●●●●●●●●●●●●●●●●●●●●●●

Somebody—I think it was me—once said: "Writing a book isn't too bad; it's the aftermath that's rough." The aftermath has its moments.

One of them is the moment of truth delivered by book reviewers. Generally speaking, a first-time author divides reviewers into two categories: 1) the brilliant, perceptive, intelligent critics who like the book, and, 2) the hoary-headed, bird-brained idiots who pan it. If a newspaper ignores the book, the author is convinced that the editor is a no-soul churl who objects to the theme for personal reasons.

My first book, *And Then There Were Eight,* was about the trials-and-tribulations-and-fun-and-games of raising eight youngsters. The second was a novel, *A Pennant for the Kremlin,* a fantasy about what might happen if, through an odd incident, the Russian government were to inherit the Chicago White Sox baseball team. Through great good luck, and with the help of fine people in the newspaper and broadcasting businesses who promoted them, both were best-sellers.

The very first review of *And Then There Were Eight* came out of New York. It was fine, but it ended with this line: "We leave the author as he is about to have his ninth child." The book suggested nothing of the sort, so I checked with Helen. She denied that she was enceinte (rather heatedly, as I recall), but a thing like that can get you off to a shaky start.

Again, one of the New York reviews about *A Pennant for the Kremlin* described me as "the well-known Chicago sports writer." This was unnerving, at first, for one who had never written a sports story in his life. But the more I thought of it, the more I saw it as a compliment.

Shaky moments occur when the author is asked to autograph his book in public. It's an honor, but it can play havoc with your nerves for there is nothing more awful than to poise—pen in hand—and suddenly realize you've drawn a blank on the names of people you've known for years. I've tried getting around this by asking: "How would you like it inscribed?" It works fine until you get this answer: "Just use my first name." At my first autographing party I became so unhinged that in the first four books I signed I got in everything (the date, good wishes, etc.) except my own name.

Once I journeyed several hundred miles to sign books in a department store that had neglected to advertise the event. There wasn't even a card in the window. Exactly three women came up to the counter where I sat in nervous isolation. One said she'd wait for the paper-back edition. The other said she'd wait for the free copy at her library, and the third—taking me for a clerk—said: "Where'd they put the hair nets? They used to be on this counter." I was so mortified by this shambles that I got up and pretended I was a shopper. Before I got out of the place I had blown nearly $20 on useless knickknacks (they had set me up near the notions department).

When his book goes well, the author must resign himself to the fact that he won't see his family for some time. For a few weeks, at least, he will spend much of his time crouched in the back seat of taxicabs, racing from one appointment to another. He will be interviewed and analyzed and investigated before small and large audiences. He will shake so many hands the lifeline will disappear from his palms, and he'll sign so many books the whole palm might just disappear. He'll consume copious amounts of hors d'oeuvres, coffee, chicken croquettes, booze, cigarette smoke, breath purifiers and bicarbonate of soda. He won't be home much, and his loved ones will have to keep track of his whereabouts on radio and television. At one point when my little Lisa greeted me with, "Hi, uncle," I decided it was time to climb off the carousel.

Making the best-seller lists will also land the author on other lists. He will get much mail from literary agents, public-speaking agencies, insurance folks, other publishers, and his creditors. A number of real estate people who read *And Then There Were Eight* were eager to sell me "just the house you need for ten people." And only $90,000. People who read of movie and musical-play options on the books have written me, pleading for roles in the project (a matter over which, of course, the author has no control). I've been asked to pose for pictures at the openings of service stations and supermarkets (I didn't) and was even requested to pose for pictures with an animal well-known in the theatrical world (I didn't get the connection either, and bowed out).

It's almost impossible for an author to pass a book store without going in to see if his book is prominently displayed. One day in New York I passed a store which—horrors!—didn't have my book in the window. I marched in, placed my brief case on a counter, and examined the shelves, but couldn't find my precious creation anywhere. When the clerk admitted he'd never heard of the title, I became livid. "This book was written by a friend of mine," I lied. "I was planning to buy four, as gifts. What kind of a stupid book store is this anyway!"

With that, I angrily snatched my brief case and there—I often wonder what color my face turned—was a healthy stack of my books which the brief case had covered up. The clerk happily slipped four copies into a bag. "That'll be $16.10," he chirped. "Drop in again."

It's the silliest feeling, buying your own book . . .

But don't get me wrong about the aftermath. Every crazy, frantic moment of it has really been sweet and wonderful.

••••••••••••••••••••••

It's a little difficult for a columnist to buckle down to work after a vacation. I was in New York City, but is that enough to write about?

I could crow that I drove all the way from Chicago to Manhattan and never once got lost. Of course it would take some talent to get lost, because in Chicago you get on the Tri-State Tollway, which falls into the Indiana Tollroad which joins with the Ohio Turnpike, which slips into the Pennsylvania Turnpike, which connects with the New Jersey Turnpike, which spills into the Lincoln Tunnel and New York City.

Not a single stoplight all the way, except at the exit from the Lincoln Tunnel. Then my luck ran out. On the very first real turn after a thousand miles I veered the wrong way and wound up in a dark, unpleasant part of the city where it's good to lock the car doors and keep your eye on St. Christopher.

In my spare time I watched some New York television, but what came across the set in my hotel room didn't lend itself much to reviews. Almost each time I'd flick it on I'd get what looked like a pretty snappy vaudeville team billed as Lefkowitz, Fino, and Gilhooley. Their jokes were all right but they were always about the same fellow—one Robert Wagner. After four days of this it occurred to me that New York was having a mayoral election.

When Lefkowitz, Fino, and Gilhooley weren't doing their buck-and-wing (don't get me wrong: I love Republicans), dozens of other politicians were going into ecstasy on the air over the delicious taste of milk. There was no milk to be had in New York, see, because of the deliverers' strike, and those fellows on the little screen were weeping about how much they missed their milk. It was a great production, but the casting was horrible because every last one of them looked like he hadn't seen a glass of milk in a dreadfully long time. I mean, some of these things were in color—and you don't get a red nose from milk.

Speaking of red noses and things like that, I was a guest on the "Today" program early one morning and before going in to chat with Frank Blair I had fifteen years taken off my face by an NBC magician who put pancake make-up where it did the most good, which, in my case, was from chin to hairline.

It happened that after the "Today" show I was due to appear on another television program (Joe Franklin's "Memory Lane") at another studio. "No use taking off the make-up," said Blair, "because you'll only have to be done up again at the other place."

So it was that I went out into the streets of New York around eight o'clock in the morning with all that make-up on, dying to hide in the back seat of a taxi. It's bad enough to wear all that goo, but at that time of day people are bound to think—uh, well, they can't help but stare if you don't look like some recognizable actor. And I couldn't find a cab.

The pancake stuff was beginning to dry up and crack a little, and I tried whistling for a taxi but little flecks of make-up kept flying out of my mouth, and there within the charcoal canyon of Rockefeller Center I sounded like a flute that's been left out in the rain for a while. And waving my arm hither and yon and looking as I did, I felt—to put it delicately—something less than masculine. At last a taxi pulled up and the first thing the man said was: "You from Miami?" I was from hunger, but I told him yes, I was from Miami.

Sadly, it was still too early for anyone to be around at Franklin's studio—the doors were still locked, for heaven's sakes—so I walked about looking for a cup of coffee. And I decided to buy a show business paper so people would think I was an actor or maybe a deodorant spieler on his way to film a television commercial, and that would explain the make-up. So I bought *Variety* and opened it wide at the center fold, so people would catch on, and the first curb I hit I fell flat on my pancake face, right in front of a subway exit—and then the people *really* stared.

You have to believe this, but there were no restaurants

open on that street where the studio was—just a bar-and-grill, and everybody in the place was sipping booze despite the hour. But I was going on the air and I asked for coffee; the fellows at the bar looked at the make-up, and a couple of them edged away to other stools. I was so nervous the coffee spilled all over my chin and ruined the make-up, and I got to the studio looking like the picture of Dorian Gray.

Now that I've come this far it just occurs to me that it was fun, all right, in New York. More important, it occurs to me that I've got my first post-vacation column out of the way—and that's always the one that doesn't come easily.

••••••••••••••••••••

I was catching up on some reading, leafing through my copy of *Fifteen Ways to Cheat at Mountain Climbing,* when the phone rang. The call was from Washington, and the man identified himself as special counsel for a Senate Subcommittee of the Judiciary.

The subcommittee for some months had been looking into the presidential nomination of Thurgood Marshall to the U.S. Circuit Court of Appeals. A Negro lawyer (who has since been appointed Solicitor General), Marshall was one of the top men in the National Association for the Advancement of Colored People, and there was some opposition to his nomination among certain southern senators.

It seems that some years ago I covered a rather strongly worded speech Marshall had made before a Negro rally in Memphis, Tennessee. Was I, the man from Washington wanted to know, that same fellow, and did I remember the incident?

I did not at the time keep clippings of my writings, a custom I adopted later when I became a columnist. But I did remember the incident.

The man from Washington asked a few more questions, then said he'd like to fly down to Chicago to see me and ask me more questions.

I explained that he'd have to come down to the suburbs because my wife was out of town, and I was at home with the eight youngsters, writing my columns from the house. He said he would.

The next day at noon he showed up at my door with an attaché case full of newspaper clippings and documents relating to Marshall and the hearings on his nomination. Among the documents were photostatic copies of my Memphis story and a transcript of Marshall's testimony before the subcommittee—in which he asserted that he had not been misquoted.

Anyway, the man was with me for two hours and all this time he fired questions at me. And toward the end I told him how much I appreciated his coming all the way down from Washington to take the deposition from me—what with my being tied down with a houseful of children and all.

With that the man from Washington reached into his attaché case and presented me with an official document which started out with the one word: "Greetings."

It was a subpoena to appear for questioning before the subcommittee at 10:30 Friday morning. This was Wednesday.

"But I can't go!" I protested. "I'd have to find a housekeeper, and there isn't much time left." The man from Washington was very polite, and he appeared to be sympathetic. But he said: "I'm afraid this is a problem you'll have to solve. You must be there at 10:30 Friday morning."

"But you've come all the way down from Washington to question me," I persisted. "You have my answers. Why do I have to go out there and start all over again?"

"I can't take a deposition from you," he said. "This was just preliminary questioning. But you have to make an act of physical presence before the subcommittee."

"What if I refuse to go? This happens to be a personal hardship case."

"I'll direct you," the man from Washington said, "to the last paragraph of the subpoena." Then he explained that I would be held in contempt of the Senate, which would mean a fine or imprisonment or both.

The subpoena, which said I was "commanded" to be in Washington, was signed by Senator James O. Eastland (Dem.-Miss.).

So it was that on that Friday morning I found myself in Washington. I found a reliable housekeeper to take over during the emergency, and I made it in time. My living expenses, transportation, and the hotel were paid by the subcommittee. When the subcommittee representative was toting up the bill, I brought up the housekeeper's pay. At first he said the government couldn't pay that. Then he said it could. The government did.

That means you, friend. Your taxes paid for the whole business.

I was on the stand before seven or eight senators exactly nine minutes, during which I answered all questions and repeated that my story had been accurate and that no editorial pressure had been brought to bear on me. The hot lights used for the television cameras made me perspire a little, but I got the impression that the senators didn't mind the hot lights and cameras one bit. Then I was excused, and each senator in turn said: "Thank you for being here."

And suddenly I felt I had come some little distance since becoming an American citizen.

••••••••••••••••••••

Herb Ruud studied the handwriting on the envelope atop the cluster of mail on his desk. There was an enticing, devil-may-care lilt in the way his name was spelled out. No question about it; the writing was feminine, even a little sensuous, and most definitely unfamiliar.

You or I wouldn't have wasted any time pondering on the sender. But Ruud is an artist—a Chicago "ghost" behind several of the popular comic strips—and a small thing like the pencraft on an envelope will intrigue an artist.

There was more—a slight fragrance of perfume wafted out of the envelope.

"Naturally, I was curious," Ruud told me as we lunched. "I opened it and out came a double-fold piece of pink stationery. Then I read the first paragraph and I felt like somebody had lit a match at the back of my neck."

He took the letter from his pocket and read it aloud:

"Perhaps I shouldn't be writing this, but I feel I just can't go on any longer without telling you that I love you."

Ruud looked up. "You can imagine how I felt," he said, with an embarrassed smile. "I got to thinking, who in the hell would—but here, you read the rest of it."

I read on: "From little things you do and say, I am certain you feel the same way about me, but you are far too noble to ever say anything.

"I realize that you are married, but let's not let that stand in the way of our happiness!"

I looked up at Ruud. "Golly," I said, "are you sure that—"

"Turn the page," he said. I did. All it said was:

"From your loving wife."

Ruud's smile was wider now, but still embarrassed. "I just had to show it to someone," he said wistfully. "It's the nicest valentine I ever got."

"How long have you been married?" I asked.

"Twenty-six years," he said.

••••••••••••••••••••••

For the next four days I would be in the hospital, undergoing a checkup. As I packed my bag, little Lisa's voice drifted through the window as she told her pals:

". . . and he's going in the hospital *right now,* and tomorrow I'm going to tell the teacher to ask the class to *pray* for him, and . . ."

I stormed outside and absolutely forbade it. She wanted to know why.

"Because everybody's going to think I'm sick," I said.

"But you *are* sick," she said.

"I am *not!* I feel wonderful!"

"Then why are you going to the hospital?"

"Because I'm—because the doctor—never mind why! Just don't tell anybody."

"You don't want us to pray for you?"

"NO! I mean—yes . . . I mean, uh, not the whole class. Just pray alone, all by yourself."

The next crisis was less unnerving. The youngsters had heard me saying that the hospital to which I was going, which is operated by the Seventh Day Adventists, does not serve meat (generally) to the patients.

"We'll bring you a baloney sandwich," trilled Nelda.

"With peanut butter," Marcia added.

I explained that children weren't allowed in the hospital. "You wave in the window and we'll throw it at you," Barbara suggested.

Actually, there was no need for (ugh) baloney-and-peanut-butter sandwiches, for I was allowed meat at the evening meal. But the religious group, whose kindness and zeal I found inspiring, recommend that protein be obtained from sources other than meat. I had entrees consisting of egg cutlets and asparagus cutlets and garbanzos and dumplings, and they were fine. They don't recommend coffee, but they took pity on an addict, and I got some.

And such efficiency! On checking in, I was taken in tow by a hostess, a volunteer worker, and within fifteen minutes I had an identification bracelet on my wrist, an X ray, a urinalysis, a blood test (I was to get plenty more of each later on) and a gift box that included a toothbrush, soap, toothpaste, a pencil, a comb, and a nail file. And that was before I even got to my room.

There I was greeted by gay little cards that had my name and messages like this: "Your doctor wants a portrait of your interior tomorrow morning. We want it to look pretty, so follow these instructions: You will be given a cathartic (and other things) after supper. You will be served a non-fat supper. Relax and enjoy it. We are all your friends. After supper, you will be treated to 'The Parade of Pills.' You take them every five minutes until all ordered have been given. They make your interior show up in the X rays. Do not eat or drink anything after midnight—not even water. Not even your regular medicine. You must not smoke. And no fair cheating."

The cards then gave interesting details about various appointments with radiologists and cardiologists and other technicians. (On the morning of the basal metabolism test, one isn't even allowed to shave, wash, or read the paper. No exertion.) And the cards urged, after each test, to: "Relax and enjoy yourself. Eat, drink, and be merry." (Until—sob—the next test.)

Now the heart. Now the lungs. Now the liver. Now the kidneys. Now the bladder. And so on. It was thorough and neat and painless (most of the time). I got a clean bill of health. But somehow I couldn't face the family without a scar or an operation or something visible to talk about.

So I asked my physician to remove a mole near my temple. He didn't cauterize it; he cut it out. And I got a nice bandage. And when I got home I told the children, with practiced nonchalance: "Minor surgery. Next week they take out the stitches." And for a moment I felt a little like a hero.

Really, though, I didn't want to tell you about my operation. Just about the simplicity and importance of a thorough checkup.

I know it costs a few dollars. But so do beer and gasoline and the golf course and the club dues and cigarettes and many other things that will be missed by the ones who depend on you much less than you will.

••••••••••••••••••••••

'Tis the season, they say, to be jolly.

Humbug. Count me out.

I've just spent half a day trying to assemble one of those put-together toys for good little boys. You know the kind—with forty-seven parts (not counting pins and wire), a dozen diagrams (with the parts concealed by sketches of big, bony fingers), and an encyclopedia of instructions that can be read only with a magnifying glass and a double shot of Old Popskull.

This one is a foreign-made spaceship complete with parachute for descent, a spaceman (also complete with parachute) and instructions that could only have been translated into English by a demented dropout.

The parts include: spaceship nose, fin for sling connections, body, balance body, free body, tubular body (anybody here seen the body?), small pivots regulating the elastic ring (which, by the way, is a rubber band) and other things like nozzles, bolts, parachute thread, and an interchangeable nose without fins (honest).

I should explain that I have a severe handicap about things like this. I have an allergy about nuts, bolts, and anything that comes in a do-it-yourself box. I have neighbors who can dismantle and reassemble their washing machines in forty minutes flat. But me—to hang up a picture I need two assistants, several blueprints, and five uninterrupted hours.

So you will understand why I didn't get much beyond the first instruction, which blithely says: "Fold parachute properly." That's all. True, there were two diagrams to go with this bulletin, but they weren't of much help (I still haven't untangled all the thread from my left wrist).

Here's more information guaranteed to bring jollity to Yuletide: "The space ship is particularly studied for not vertical launching, but for launching slanted up to 30 degrees from the ground . . . At the top of its flight the free body automatically opens rendering free the parachute . . . It is possible setting the space man with its own parachute inside the space ship" (possible, ha!).

Don't give up, I told myself. Stay with it.

The instructions continue: "The free body is automatically controlled by a special device which releases the parachute, nearly when the space ship is at the top of its fly. This device is composed by balance, bolt, elastic ring" (maybe the device is composed, but I'm not).

There's more: "When the space ship is at the top trajectory the already-named physical actions, force of gravity, aerodynamic action, are such that the ring strength prevails and shifts the bolt which the outer arm hinders no more so that the space ship may open. The height it might reach, with equal trowing impulse, depends on the elastic ring tension corresponds to higher working security but also causes the free body to open a little in advance" (I am NOT making this up).

The last instruction is great. It warns you to launch the thing "in areas free of people since you would not be sure of how to use it." That's an understatement if I've ever read one.

Let's see, now. Where's the counter with the basketballs?

•••••••••••••••••••••

I have just been psychoanalyzed. Care to join me on the couch?

The analysis came in the mail, unsolicited, from a reader who happens to be a psychologist with a Ph.D. after his name and a distaste for my columns. The trouble with me, he writes, is that I'm too emotional and fixated in the oral stage. He adds:

"This . . . may also explain why your editors or you, consciously or unconsciously, selected a picture of *your drinking a cup of coffee* as the heading on top of your column."

I didn't realize that dark, psychological symbols lurk behind the candid photo used with the column for years. But the doctor's sex-oriented letter was two pages long, and the shock sent me riffling nervously through other photos that accumulate in this business. I tell you it's madness. Weird symbols all over the place.

In some old files I found a picture of Perry Como and me in deep conversation at an affair in New York. We were discussing Kraft at the time, I think, though I don't remember if it was Kraft Cheese or Krafft-Ebing. The significant thing is that a cigarette holder is clenched between my teeth. Heavens to hallucinations, there's a symbol for you.

In this connection, I also found a picture of me following Sir Winston Churchill with a notebook and pencil in my hand during the Quebec Conference. I don't even have a cigarette in this one, but Sir Winston has a cigar. How about *that,* doctor?

In another photo, I'm at a party with Rochester of the Jack Benny program, and there's a small live pig on our table. (It would take too long to explain what the pig was doing there.) I venture that some psychologists would say that the fixation, in this case, was on the camera: We were hogging it.

This find-the-fixation is intriguing. Here's a picture with Jack Bailey showing the crown he used on his program, "Queen For A Day" (laurel fixation?). Here's another with actor Jim Garner helping me mount a horse (known as galloping fixation). And another with Lawrence Welk at lunch (because of his ulcers Welk's diet sometimes consists of strained baby foods, and anyone worth his Ph.D. can figure a dandy angle on that one).

And so it goes. Here I am under a tree on a California ranch with Richard Boone, each of us with a can of beer (Schlitzophrenia?). Here's another shot with Adolphe Menjou trying on a vest in a Beverly Hills tailor shop (the transvestite wish).

Since the psychologist rattled my nerves with his diagnosis, I'll rattle his with these sinister exhibits: a picture with Betty Grable, she with both eyes shut tightly (couldn't stand the sight of me?). With Danny Thomas, arm in arm (the father Emmyge). With Liberace, sipping bubbly (latent dipsosis, also known as the champagne complex). With Buster Keaton, eating pie (Soupy Sales syndrome). With

Gene Barry, me fingering his tie (a rare attachment marked by an odd craving for cravats), and me holding a cat (the classic Oedipuss complex).

And, oh, here's a cutie: I'm sitting on a World War I cannon in Canada, and it's facing south—aimed at the United States (this was before I entered this country as an alien). It's an interesting coincidence that the late Walter Cannon, a Harvard psychologist, made his mark as an expert on the automatic nervous system.

And here I am autographing one of my books in a department store (acute narcissism). Asleep at the typewriter (hidden death wish). With young singer Tommy Sands, him holding a mallet (never mind me, Doc; what's with the mallet bit?). And a double exposure with George Gobel (dual personality neurosis).

But the photo that should delight the psychologist is the one which accompanies this column, along with the coffee-cup picture. It was taken when I was five years old and I recall the furious fight I put up against posing in those miserable rompers. I thought I looked like—shucks—a girl. That's when I started hating the world, and I screamed until I was blue in the face.

Especially around the nose.

••••••••••••••••••••••

At last I'm vindicated. I am neither a coward nor a nut, as I feared. A bit of a freak, yes, but apart from that I'm all right. It's a great feeling.

It all started years ago when I discovered I couldn't float in the water. I tried everything, but the results, dismally, were always the same. I sank like a stone.

For hours on end I'd watch the others lazying around on

their backs or treading water—and how I envied them. I told myself it was all in the head, and kept on practicing. Not a chance. Glub—right to the bottom. In my time, I've swallowed enough water to float a battleship.

It's hard to describe the anguished frustration of the sinker. At the pool, I've had to confine myself to the shallow end, threshing splashily around amid three-year-olds like a drunken dolphin. It's pretty embarrassing to have to wade to poolside and ask some strange lady if you can borrow her child's water-wings.

All these years, friends and relatives—my own family, for heaven's sake—have sneered and snickered when I tried explaining I couldn't float. Babies can float. Dogs can float. Me? Bottoms up and gurgle-gurgle.

But the other afternoon at a country club I found a merciful, long-awaited exoneration. I emerged from the pool, gasping and choking as usual, and confronted the club's swimming coach, John Marcy. "It's no use," I wheezed, my lungs bursting, "I'll never make it. I'm a sinker."

"I'm one too," said Marcy.

This was unbelievable. For years Marcy was a professional diver in New York and, in 1957, placed third in the national collegiate championships. But it was true. "Unless I make sculling motions with my hands," said Marcy, "down I go."

What blessed relief! Since then I've talked with others who have this problem. One of them is William Peterson, swimming coach at Northwestern University since 1943. "I used to be a sinker," he confessed, "but in recent years I've put on a little weight and now I can float."

Another sinker is Jim Moran, the local automobile tycoon and a real water buff who swims an hour each day. "I go down like a rock," he admits.

Marcy and Peterson tell me that it has to do with the body make-up. People who are big-boned and heavy-muscled simply don't displace as much water as others, and they sink. Some authorities call this "negative buoyancy," which does not afflict women at all. Nor does it afflict men who have a little extra fat (the fatter you are, naturally, the easier you float).

I spoke with Adolph Kiefer, holder of many swim records who was the Olympic backstroke champion back in 1936. "About one out of one thousand individuals are sinkers," he said. "There's a theory that larger bones mean more bone marrow, and that extra weight works against normal buoyancy."

I checked this with some medical authorities, but the doctors didn't want to commit themselves on the marrow theory (on the average, one's marrow weighs about as much as one's liver). But generally they agreed that if you're lean and muscular and big-boned, you won't be much of a floater—if at all. Some of us are afflicted more than others; even when I paddle arms and legs, I sink.

Peterson tells me that football players are notorious sinkers because of their build.

In any event, it's consoling to learn that inability to float is just one of nature's oddities, and I hope the news will encourage other non-floaters to take heart. I'm so delighted I feel like I'm floating on air.

But I do wish I could say the same for the water.

•••••••••••••••••••••

I just hope I don't have an accident this week.

You know how it is when you faint on the street or get hit by a car. They go through your pockets and all that, looking for identification. If something happens to me I know I'll die—of massive embarrassment. For in my pockets, chances are, they'll find a compact—complete with powder puff. And a thing like that can kill you.

It all started last weekend when I returned from New York where I'd appeared on some television and radio programs to talk about a book I had written (*A Pennant for the Kremlin*). When I reached home I asked the children how they had liked Old Dad on television.

"You sure have big bags under your eyes," Georgia said.

I asked Shonagh if she'd seen me on NBC's "Today" program. "That Hugh Downs," she sighed, rolling her eyes skyward, "is the cutest thing."

I turned to Nelda. "I was on 'To Tell the Truth,'" I said, trying to keep calm. "Did I look all right?"

"You kept putting your hand in front of your face," said Nelda, proving that everybody's a critic these days.

"That's to hide the bags under his eyes," said Marcia, who—sadly—was probably right.

I explained to the brood that the large black circles under my eyes were a family trait. My mother had noticeably deep circles, though I must say that on her they looked good. But the kids wouldn't buy that.

Then I explained that at my age all people have bags under their eyes. They retorted that Downs and the others they saw on the programs seemed totally unbagged.

"But they had make-up!" I shouted. "They're stars, and they're important."

Little Lisa looked up from a drawing. "Daddy's not important," she mused.

"I wouldn't say that," I said. "Remember two years ago when I was on television in New York? They put make-up on me then."

"Maybe you're not important any more," somebody—I forget who—said. It was an awful setback, but at least it ended the painful discussion.

Now about the powder puff bit: This week I'm to appear on the "Lee Phillip Show" and I'll be a panelist on Irv Kupcinet's conversation program. So I called Miss Phillip, coughed the panic out of my voice, and asked if her guests were ever adorned with make-up.

"A make-up man on standby costs $100," Miss Phillip explained, "so we don't make people up unless they're very important, and they insist."

There was a long, mortifying silence on both ends of the line.

I ventured that sometimes my bags look like a pair of kangaroo pouches. "In that case," Miss Phillip offered, "I'll put something on. I'll fix your eyes myself."

The thought of a pretty young lady erasing the lines of time off my face made me ill.

"Never mind," I said, in the show-must-go-on tradition. "Just pan the cameras on my left ear. It's quite normal."

"Don't give it a thought," Miss Phillip said. "Make-up doesn't really do very much anyway."

When I put the phone down I wondered if she meant that personally.

I got in touch with Kupcinet's producer, Paul Frumkin. He, too, said that make-up was out.

"What if I insist?" I countered.

"It'll be a good show," he said casually. "We have six or seven very interesting guests." I got the point.

Frumkin added: "Once an old-time actress insisted on make-up. Terribly fussy person." Again I got the point.

Anyway, I hope the studio doormen don't stop me when I show up on those programs with a powder puff bulge in my pocket. And I've ordered the children to watch the Kupcinet program, because it happens that Hugh Downs—who's in town—will be on that program too.

Let's see what *he* looks like without make-up.

•••••••••••••••••••••

One cold night last month I drove ninety miles to address the annual dinner of a tri-city chamber of commerce. As I neared the hotel where the affair was taking place, I saw a large group of men on the street waving their arms and directing me where to park.

What a warm reception, I thought, but they didn't have to come out in the cold. I was doubly touched when the leader of the street delegation turned out to be the president of the chamber and an executive of a bank in the area. This really is a warm reception, I thought again.

It was all of that. The hotel, the chamber president explained, was on fire.

It wasn't a disaster, but something had gone wrong in the kitchen and the chamber's 285 steaks had been destroyed. The firemen had evacuated the hotel because of heavy smoke and water.

I have a return engagement at the chamber's postponed dinner when I hope the main course will consist of cold cuts. But such, sometimes, are the perils of public speaking.

Odd things tend to happen on the lecture circuit. Like showing up for a talk on the wrong night or getting lost out of town and arriving as the audience is heading for the coat rack. Once I got to a church auditorium to find the people friendly enough, but somewhat hesitant about where I was to sit on the stage. There was some discreet coughing all around, then I discovered there was no chair for me on the stage. Wrong church. I was due at another church of another denomination in another block.

On another occasion I was in the right place but gave the wrong speech. I was announced as speaking on a certain subject but got my signals crossed and did an hour on a theme not billed on the program. Only when I was through did I realize why madam chairman was such a foot-tapper.

But most madam chairmen I've met have been kind souls, including those who insist on pinning a carnation to your lapel before you go onstage. The trouble with this kindness is you put your head down to organize your thoughts and your nose dips into the aromatic petals and—well, there's nothing worse than a monumental sneeze to blow what might have been a good line.

Sadly, I'm prone to mechanical hazards. I can never adjust the microphone after a four-foot or six-foot introducer has turned it over to me, and just as I give up on the knobs a ninety-pound bit of a woman will come up onstage and fix it. All you can do is stand there looking exactly as you feel, helpless and stupid.

The odds are high that some time during your talk the sound system will go kaput or the air-conditioning unit will come on like Niagara or the radiators will start knocking like xylophones gone mad. On other nights, everything is quiet and you feel just great and just as you reach that brilliant punch line, an obscene jet zooms overhead and annihilates it.

The introduction routine can be unnerving. Once I was introduced with the wrong first name (Tom), the wrong second name (O'Malley) and—I take an oath on this—the wrong newspaper. And this from the president of a Rotary Club. Another time, moments before going on, the fellow who was to introduce me invited me into the men's room so he could question me and make notes for his speaker's introduction. I didn't mind his lack of preparation too much, but one does feel silly—standing in a men's room and telling a stranger the story of one's life.

Once a pre-talk business session droned on and on, and it was ten o'clock when I was introduced. "It's been a long, tiresome night," the well-meaning lady started, "but it's not over yet. We have with us tonight . . ."

For some reason that escapes me there seems to be a feeling among some program chairmen that newspaper columnists loathe money and would be insulted by a speaker's fee. Museum curators, people who collect antique clocks, and fashion co-ordinators apparently have no trouble getting paid, but columnists often are expected to leave their loved ones for a night or a whole day, sometimes traveling a good distance, and be thrilled with a vote of thanks.

A program chairman once told me: "We have a speakers' budget, but we only use that for doctors and psychiatrists." To this day, this policy eludes me.

Another time a program chairman told me that her Chicago club only paid out-of-town speakers. "But I'm from out of town," I said. "I live in the suburbs." Her good-by was unmistakably cool.

On yet another occasion a program chairman said her group did not pay speakers, but my appearance would be "wonderful publicity" for me. "Your picture," she went on, "will be in our local paper and it has a circulation of more than 2000!"

There wasn't enough fight left in me to tell her that my picture appears in The Chicago *Sun-Times* every day, a newspaper whose weekday circulation is heading toward the 600,000 mark.

But my favorite lady chairman is the one who asked if

she could tape-record my talk. Making a silly joke, I said fine—if I got the residuals.

"Of course," she beamed. "I'll make copies and send you one."

••••••••••••••••••••••

It's a terrible feeling—to suddenly discover that you can't write any more. It has just happened to me.

Oh, I can still put one little word behind another and come up with an acceptable sentence. What I mean is I'm finding it difficult to write by hand. After twenty years of using a typewriter for almost every writing need, a person becomes dreadfully rusty with pen and pencil.

It all started in December when my family let it be known that my Christmas present, this time, would be a new typewriter. I was given my choice of machine, and, since I wasn't going to pay for it, I chose a German job.

I put in the order and gave my old typewriter—the one I use at home—to my son. That was his Christmas present, and he took it away with him to college. Then I sat back and waited for my new machine.

And waited. And waited.

I've been waiting for more than three months, and I still don't have it. The dock-workers' strike interfered with delivery, and, last time I checked, the typewriter was still sitting somewhere in a ship's hold in New York.

Meanwhile I had to go back to a ball-point pen for the writing I do at home. And my writing now, it turns out, is awful. The "q" looks like a "g" or a "y," the "r" looks like an "n" or a "v," and the "f" looks like a disabled horsefly.

One night, when I came home late, I left a note for the children to wake me at six in the morning. They called me at eight, because that's the way they read it in the note. Every one of them.

On another occasion I left a note for the milkman, advising him we would need no milk next day. Not only did he leave four gallons, but he left two pints of cottage cheese and a quart of eggnog (in March, yet).

In the last month alone five of my checks have been returned. The recipients made out my signature all right, but they couldn't tell how much they were getting.

Once, when we kept one of our daughters home from school because of illness, I wrote her teacher a note, explaining that the child had the flu. The teacher wrote back that she appreciated my letter, but why was my child absent from school?

The ultimate in this frustration occurred last weekend when I wrote myself a grocery list and went to the supermarket. I found I couldn't read my own writing and came home laden down with things like canned chili con carne, frozen frogs' legs and four tins of cat meat—staples that have never been in the house before. What's more, we don't have a cat.

I dearly hope my Christmas present arrives soon. I'm just too old to start over again with penmanship. And besides, I'm terribly tired of frozen frogs' legs.

••••••••••••••••••••

"Bless us, O Lord, and these thy gifts," the children said as they started grace at dinner not long ago. Because she was standing near little Lisa at the time, my wife, Helen, caught her odd interpretation of the prayer: "Bless us, O Lord," Lisa trilled, "and be my guest."

Because the invitation seemed so appropriate, I guess I

shall always remember Lisa's fluff. For all of us, there are sounds that will always remain, and most of them are echoes from the distant past. Why do they keep returning? It can't be because we wish to return to that past—because not all of those sounds are happy ones.

I remember so vividly, for instance, the voice of the doctor outside my hospital room one night when I was sixteen. He was telling my father: "It's rheumatic fever, all right. He'll have to stay here quite a while." It must have been the stern tone of his voice, because I recall little else from my stay.

And what man can forget his first real job? "You can start Monday," the editor said, "at $19.50 a week."

I remember the very first funeral I was taken to. It must have been someone close because I stood by the grave with my parents, and I remember—to the point where I often hear it again—the strange whirring noise in the morning sun as the casket slid slowly downward.

I remember—perhaps because it was so often—my wife saying: "You'd better call the doctor . . . I think it's time." And a few hours later the doctor saying: "You have another girl" (good grief—again!). I remember, a very long time ago, running into the living room, shrieking: "Look at my shoelaces! I tied them—alone!" I guess I had expected a heroic hurrah, but all that happened was my brother grunting: "It's about time."

I remember waking in my parents' bed and my father saying: "It's all right. The tonsils are out now." (In those days the operation was often performed in your house, on the kitchen table.) And doesn't the sound of the recess bell in the schoolyard come back to you too?

I remember, still in dread, the awesome noise of the little plane on my first flight. I was alone with a bush pilot over the Canadian far north and below us was nothing but frozen white wilderness . . . And more recently, I remember the sound of the airliner that plunged into a cornfield I could see from my window.

I remember being sent on my first interview—a fellow called Lawrence Tibbett and a singer named Grace Moore at the airport (who were they?) . . . And who can forget the voice of the child who comes in, repentant after punishment, to whisper: "I'm sorry . . ."

And I remember Mark straggling into the kitchen, his drawers at his ankles, to announce: "I went to the baf'room! I went to the baf'room! BY MYSELF!!!"

I remember walking through a hospital and hearing some child, in a faraway room, whimpering over and over: "I want to go home . . ." And the man must be rare who can forget the first time he heard these words: "We feel you've earned a little raise . . ." I remember, as a miner, the fearsome sound of cracking twigs as I walked to the mineshaft by myself through the bush each dawn, certain that a bear was stalking me . . . And I don't think I shall ever forget the tone of my son's voice when he telephoned me at the office one night: "Guess what? We won, but wait a minute—I hit three for four."

I remember the ice cracking like a wild whip over the lake at the nearness of spring, a wild, awesome sound that reminded me a little of thunder, and the roar of the flood waters destroying the first home we ever owned.

They often wake me, those special sounds, in the stillness of the night. Do yours?

I suppose that in some way we all yen for yesteryear. Now that school is out, for example, I can't help recalling the ways in which we amused ourselves during summer vacation. They're more elaborate and glamorous—and expensive—today, but I suspect that yesterday's child had more fun, perhaps because he was less organized and made up in ingenuity what he lacked in equipment.

It all came back the other day when I bought a swing-and-trapeze set for the back yard. Do other middle-agers remember the old tire at the end of a rope dangling from a tree branch? Some days, with enough momentum, you could actually see the horizon.

Does anyone else recall the quickening of the pulse when the ice wagon came lumbering down the street, and you knew the man would let you on to gather a handful of chips? And the vegetable wagon? I don't know about your children, but at least two of mine have never seen a horse. Today? Motorized popsicles and a buck and a half for the runt pack the bell lures in.

Does anybody remember kick-the-can on the street? In those days, you could play on the street at least five minutes before a car came along. Today? Little League Baseball in a manicured park.

Getting sprayed by the neighbor's hose was really something to talk about. Today it's I'm-tired-of-your-pool-let's-go-in-my-pool.

We were lucky. There actually was a lagoon near where we lived—a dirty, abandoned lagoon green with algae and alive with frogs. And each summer we built a raft and gondoliered around our stinking sea until sunset. Today's child can't possibly near that thrill, even if his father sports a skiff.

There was also a dairy near our house. I mean a real dairy with real cows, and at day's end we'd go there when the milk wagons clomped back from their runs to watch the horses being led to their stalls for the night. Then we'd carry home a pail of buttermilk, courtesy of the management which used to throw away rivers of it nightly. Today? Fifteen cents a glass, and it tastes like nothing.

Remember the home-made scooters, with a couple of old wheels and a few slats of wood? And the fun to be found in the simple things . . . Cooking raw potatoes to an absolute black in a small fire by the river bank. Today? Barbecue grills, and the sissies hide their hands in asbestos . . . Putting on plays in the garage (Admishan–2 sent). Today? Television in the twilight of the living room . . . A penny's worth of candy shopping at the grocery store, where a penny got you enough to half-fill a bag. And those glorious pennies came from scouring the garbage cans for empty bottles . . . Today? Allowances–in paper money yet . . . In wintertime, sliding down the hill in cardboard cartons. Today: "Here's a sturdy toboggan–only $29.95."

And on Sundays at dusk, to the band concert in the park where you sneaked away to spy on the old people necking in the bushes.

It was all so long ago, yet it remains so vivid. One wonders what today's child will remember when his turn comes.